Back₁ o
SouthEast Asia

Tips for visiting Cambodia, Laos, Thailand, and Vietnam

By Anton Swanepoel

BACKPACKING
SOUTHEAST ASIA

Tips for Visiting Cambodia, Laos,
Thailand, and Vietnam

ANTON SWANEPOEL

Anton Swanepoel

http://antonswanepoelbooks.com/
http://antonswanepoelbooks.com/blog/
http://www.facebook.com/AuthorAntonSwanepoel
https://twitter.com/Author_Anton

Follow this link if you want updates on new book releases by the Author. http://antonswanepoelbooks.com/subscribe.php
For travel tips follow his blog.

Table of Contents

Introduction...4
Chapter 1: Initial Planning 5
Chapter 2: How Much Will It Cost? 8
Chapter 3: When To Go...10
Chapter 4: Visas 12
Chapter 5: What To Take...19
Chapter 6: What To Leave at Home....................................26
Chapter 7: Bag Selection 29
Chapter 8: Immunization..32
Chapter 9: Health 38
Chapter 10: Money Matters..45
Chapter 11: Dressing Up 52
Chapter 12: Travel Insurance 55
Chapter 13: Language Problems 56
Chapter 14: Accommodations 58
Chapter 15: Bed Bugs..64
Chapter 16: Transportation..67
Chapter 17: Internet and Cell Phone Service 73
Chapter 18: Etiquette...77
Chapter 19: Saving Money On Your Trip 81
Chapter 20: You and the Law; How to Stay Out of Jail...........84
Chapter 21: Scams to Watch Out For 91
Chapter 22: Volunteering 98
Chapter 23: Safety..100
About the Author...105
More Books by Anton...106

Introduction

Note, this book is not a travel guide to South East Asia.

This book gives tips and advice for visiting Cambodia, Laos, Thailand, and Vietnam. Although the advice is applicable to most travelers, the book is directed towards backpackers.

The advice in this book is to help you plan and pack for your trip. It is also intended to help travelers stay safe on the road, avoid common scams, and save money while having as much fun as possible.

The information provided covers scenarios and problems you may encounter when backpacking, and comes from my 30 years of experience traveling the world. At the time of this writing, I have backpacked for over 18 months though Cambodia, Laos, Thailand, and Vietnam. In addition, I have motorcycled all over Cambodia, including the Ho Chi Ming Road from Hanoi to Saigon. I have also incorporated tips from fellow travellers that I have picked up along the way.

Backpacking South-East Asia is one of the most wonderful things one can do, let me help you prepare for your adventure.

Disclaimer

Although the advice in the book is from my own experience, I cannot guarantee nothing will happen on your trip, nor that you will have exactly the same results as I had. Backpacking is and adventure – go with the flow.

Although prices were correct at the time of this writing, governments have the right to change their visa fees and visa lengths without notice.

Chapter 1: Initial Planning

Your heart is beating wildly and emotions tear at you. Fear and joy have a tug of war with your heart. The sheer excitement of a backpacking adventure is intoxicating. However, the fear of not knowing what to expect can derail plans and have people put off their dreams – or worse – cancel them.

If this is your first trip…relax. It really is not difficult, and is not the Wild West or jungles filled with booby traps. There is, in reality, only one thing you need for your adventure – a will to travel. A spirit for excitement, and discovering the unknown, will help in the start, but even that, you will obtain on your journey.

Money, passport, visas, airplane tickets and so forth, all come by themselves when you put your mind to travel. All you have to do is decide to go, and find solutions for what is holding you back. I know people that went to Asia with a one-way ticket and $200 in their pocket, and now permanently live there and own their own business. The sky is no longer the limit; your imagination is.

First Things First – What To See
To see South-East Asia, you could backpack your entire life, and not see it all. There will always be another cave, temple, island, waterfall, or some attraction that you missed or that just opened when you are about to head home.

The first thing you should do is prioritize the most important things, or places, you want to see in the countries you want to visit. Working out a budget and length of stay, is a crapshoot, at best, without having some idea of what places you want to visit.

If you have loads of cash and time, you can just take your passport and go for it. However, few people are so fortunate. Proper planning will make the most of your trip, even if you plan to backpack through Asia for a year. Without planning, you may blow through your money in a few months, or end your gap year, missing many of the things you wanted to see. One of the worst ways to plan is to say you will backpack until your money runs out. This is a sure way to end your trip in a bar, having seen very little, or worse, ending up a drug addict.

Take the places you want to see and write them down in order of importance, with the minimum days needed to visit each attraction. If you have no idea what you want to see, have a look at my mini guides for the top 20 attractions in each city for:

http://www.antonswanepoelbooks.com/cambodia.php
http://www.antonswanepoelbooks.com/laos.php
http://www.antonswanepoelbooks.com/thailand.php
http://www.antonswanepoelbooks.com/vietnam.php

Once you have a list, you will have a rough itinerary and an idea how long you need to plan to travel. At this stage, you may realize your holiday is too short to accommodate all the attractions you would like to see. You may need to extend your holiday, or sadly, cut your list. Remember to add one day for travel between major cities, such as Siem Reap and Phnom Penh in Cambodia, as well as between countries such as going from Bangkok to Siem Reap or Phnom Penh to Saigon.

I suggest you do not plan too tightly, unless you have only three days to travel. When backpacking in Asia, you will soon realize that buses are not always reliable, tuk tuks do sometimes forget to pick you up, and you may oversleep and miss your bus, after a late night out.

Ideally, to see any of these countries properly and experience the local culture, you should plan on a month per country, keeping in mind a week as a minimum. If you only have a week of vacation, then I suggest seeing only one country, or maybe two. The only worthwhile one-week two-country vacation I suggest is two days in Bangkok, and three days in Siem Reap, with two days of travel (Bangkok-Siem Reap-Bangkok).

Following are the minimums I suggest for the major towns:

Cambodia

Siem Reap - three days.
Kampot and Sihanoukville - two days each.
Phnom Penh, Battambang, and Kep - each one day.

Vietnam

Hanoi - three days.
Hoi An, Phnong Nha, and Hue - two days each.
Da lat, and Siagon - one day each.

Thailand

Bangkok, Pattaya and Chai Mai - two days each.
Ayutthaya - one day, or two days if seeing 'The Big Buddha' as well.

Laos

Vientiane, and 4000 islands - two days each.

Now that you have an idea of what you want to see, you can start planning your budget.

Chapter 2: How Much Will It Cost?

Budgeting for a backpacking trip through South-East Asia is actually easier than it sounds. Depending on how long you are traveling, one of your biggest expensive will actually be getting to your first place, and then getting back home. Depending on where you live, a flight could be as little as $300, or as much as $3000.

To get into South-East Asia, I suggest flying to Bangkok, and then taking buses or minivans from there. Bangkok is one of the most visited cities in the world, and flights are plentiful from all over the globe. They may also prove to be a lot cheaper than flying to the neighboring countries. However, if you are on a tight schedule, the day or so lost in travel will be worth more than the added price to fly direct to perhaps Siem Reap in Cambodia or Hanoi in Vietnam. I use *http://www.expedia.com/* for my flight bookings, but do not always follow their suggested routes. Try flying to different cities and make up your own route to save money.

Once you have budgeted for your transport costs, the next item is accommodations. Cambodia is currently the cheapest, with Vietnam one of the more expensive places. As a benchmark, you can count on around $5 a day for a dorm room in Laos, Thailand, and Cambodia (some go for $3 a day, but I would suggest spending the extra $2). In Vietnam, homestay is around $5 a day, but there is not much available in all the towns. Anticipate more for around $10 a day. In Cambodia, Thailand, Laos, and Vietnam, for $10 to $15 a day, you can get a double bed, air-conditioned bedroom. A fan only room is around $8 to $12, depending on how close to the city the hotel is.

For food, you can get street food for approximately $1 to $2 in all the countries. A more upmarket meal (burger) goes for around $4 to $5. A meal in a nicer restaurant will set you back $10 to $15.

Drafts go for a dollar or less, depending on the place, and coffee, tea, and sodas are roughly a $1. Water is around 50c for 500ml, and 1.5L going for 0.75c to $2, depending on where you buy.

I would suggest you plan on a minimum of $10 accommodation a day, and $15 a day for food. This should give you some leeway. You can bring this amount down considerably if you shop in local markets and cook for yourself.

With these calculations, you will need to add in Visa costs (about $60 a month), as well as transport costs and expenses for seeing attractions. As the attractions are so many and vast, I would suggest you look up what entrance fees are for each attraction. It can add up quickly; such as Angkor Wat is $40 for three days (minimum suggested). Transport cost between towns depends on how much you want to travel; however, for around $120 you can travel from Phnom Penh to Siem Reap (Cambodia), then to Vientiane (Laos), on to Bangkok (Thailand) and then make it back to Siem Reap. Add another $20 and you can make it to Saigon (Vietnam) and add about $50 you can ride the train to Hanoi (Vietnam's capital).

In real life, things rarely go as planned, thus I would suggest a minimum of $500 a month if you have backpacked before and intend on sharing rooms or staying in hostels. If you have not backpacked before or will be traveling alone, I suggest a minimum budget of $1000 a month.

Note, if you are staying a few months, you can rent a room from a local, and live on $500 a month in Cambodia; however, it will take some sacrifice. Regardless of your budget, I suggest having at least a $500 emergency fund. Remember, these amounts are suggested minimums for backpackers. If you want to eat in expensive restaurants and stay in nice hotels, you are going to need a lot more money. The suggestions do not include binge drinking every night, nor what you will spend on souvenirs or sightseeing. You have to add in guides, as well as taxi fares.

Guides are generally $20 a day or more, and a tuk tuk can set you back at least $15 for a half day. If you are only coming for a month, I would suggest a minimum of $1000 for sightseeing alone. If you are coming for a few months, then you can bring it down to around $500 a month, as you will tend to stay longer in the same spot.

Chapter 3: When To Go

The right time to go is right now – failing that – when you can. Still, there are a few things to keep in mind. Around major holidays such as Christmas and New Year, prices do tend to go up, but are still reasonable. During the hot season, it may be uncomfortable to be out all day seeing temples, consider going at a cooler time. During the wet season, the countryside turns lush green, and some of the temples are often covered in plant growth. However, you may lose a day or two when everything gets rained out, and distant temples may be unreachable due to gravel roads that become impassable mud roads.

If you are planning boat rides down the rivers, the wet season is a better bet, as many rivers get too low for boats to negotiate in the dry season.

Be advised that if you suffer from heart problems or cannot take extreme heat, travel in the cooler, rainy season, or relax during the hot part of the day. It is also important to drink plenty of water, and you may consider bunking with someone to get an air-conditioned room.

Cool, Rainy Season: October to the end of November.
Cool Season: December to Mid-March.
Hot Season: Mid-March to the end of June.
Hot, Rainy Season: The end of June to September, although by the end of July it is far cooler.

Wet Season
The wet season is from May to October, with July to September being the peak, rainy months.

During this time, the wet southwest monsoons blow in, and a large portion of the annual rainfall occurs. During the peak rainy season, roads get flooded and may become impassable (if dirt roads). Things are, however, cheaper during this time, and if you cannot stand the heat, this is the time to come. The coastal areas get rough seas, so swimming may be out on some days. Yet, the country really turns green and the bird life explodes (as do the insects).

Dry Season

The dry season runs from November (coolest) to April (hottest), with November to January being cooler and February to April being hot and dusty.

During this time, a dusty, northeast monsoon arrives. November to January is nice and cool, and then things heat up. By April, it can easily go into the high 30's – with the humidity, making it feel like the low 40s at times.

People tend to avoid the rain, causing the hot season to be the peak tourist season, with the drier months (November to January) being the busiest.

See the following website for weather forecasts before and during your trip *http://www.wunderground.com/*.

Chapter 4: Visas

For all four countries, you will need a passport that is valid for at least six months from the day you intend on entering a country. If you plan on backpacking for a while, note that a visa extension may be denied if your passport is valid less than six months when you apply for a visa renewal. Visa prices online and in guidebooks, are often wrong, as fees change without notice. Also be aware, prices may vary due to corruption occurring at smaller, land-border posts.

Note that most visas take up an entire page, as does a visa extension. Thus, backpacking for a few months can easily fill up your passport. If you need to get a new passport, ask for a maxi passport. These passports normally have around 48 pages. Alternatively, if you are low on pages, you may be able to go to your consulate and ask them to add more pages to your passport.

You will need at least two blank pages per visa, as well as visa extension (one page for the visa and one page for the entry stamps). Thailand land-border crossing is only a stamp. Tip - bring a black pen with you to the border.

Cambodia

Cambodia is perhaps the easiest country to obtain a visa. There are currently two types of visas available: a Tourist Visa, and a Business Visa (called E visa). Talk of a Student Visa, and Retirement Visa, have been going on for some time, but nothing has happened at the time of this book's writing. It used to be very easy to get a Business Visa that was valid for 3, 6, or 12 months, but it is getting harder and harder now with new laws and stricter requirements.

Tourist Visa

A tourist Visa at the time of this writing cost $30 + $7 processing fee, and can easily be obtained at all border crossings, with Siem Reap and Phnom Penh airport being the easiest locations.

Note: Ko Kong crossing can be a problem, having a lot of scams and a very poor exchange rate from Baht to Riel (officers may demand you pay in Baht). The Tourist Visa is valid for 30 days from arrival. You can renew your visa once while in Cambodia, after that, you will need to leave Cambodia and come back again. Renewal is around $45 to $55 depending on the tourist agency you use.

To make things easier at border crossings, get an online visa beforehand. This is especially useful for the Poipet border between Thailand and Cambodia (Bangkok to Siem Reap route). The cost is $40 total, including processing fees and can be paid online with a Visa or Master Card. Approval normally takes three working days, and a confirmation email will be emailed to you. Print two copies of the visa, and take it directly to the immigration desk.

Note: for online visas, you will need a passport with more than six months remaining beyond your intended time of entry, and a recent passport-size photo in digital format (JPEG or PNG format). In addition, online visas are not accepted at small border crossings. The visa is valid for three months from the day you specified you want to enter, so if you are a few days late – no worries. However, the visa can be extended only once for 30 days, up to the expiring date of the visa. Thus if you enter two months after the visa was granted, it cannot be extended in Cambodia, and you will need to leave the country.

See *https://www.evisa.gov.kh/*
For an iPhone visa application app, see:
https://itunes.apple.com/us/app/cambodia-e-visa/id859901546?ls=1&mt=8
For an android visa application app, see:
https://play.google.com/store/apps/details?id=com.e_visa

Note: it is very difficult and expensive to get a Work Visa after you initially acquire a Tourist Visa. If you want to stay and work in Cambodia, get a Work Visa from the start. Else, you will be doing endless border runs.

Business Visa

A Business Visa at the time of writing cost $35 + $7 processing fee, and is only available at the two major airports in Siem Reap and Phnom Penh. They are also available at your country's consular services or at consular services in the listed towns above. Some travelers report getting a Business Visa, without a work permit, for their first year at the Poipet border, but most are denied unless you have paperwork and a work permit.

Your initial visa is valid for 30 days from arrival. You can renew your Business Visa indefinitely for periods of 1, 3, 6, or 12 months. The 6 and 12-month visas are multi-entry visas, so if you plan on leaving and entering Cambodia, get the 6 or 12-month visa. If not, your visa will expire when you leave the country. At the time of writing, a full one-year Business Visa costs around $280 (agents may add a few bucks but should still be under $300). Bring four passport sized color pictures.

You have to leave the country and cancel your previous visa if you want to change visa groups, such as going from a Tourist Visa to a Business Visa.

Renewing Cambodia Visas

Renewing a visa is very easy in Cambodia. Any tour company can arrange that for you, and just about any hotel or guesthouse. Stay with larger tour companies and larger guesthouses where there are more backpackers. Processing normally takes around three to five days.

You will need one passport sized color photo for your visa and your current passport with your previous visa. If you do not have a picture, some will take a scan of your passport picture for a fine of $1, however, not all do it, so keep a picture with you.

For a Business Visa, you will not need a work permit for the first year. However, the second year, you will need a work permit that, at the time of writing, cost $100 + between $25 and $50 processing fees. You will also need to back pay for the first year that you were in Cambodia on a Business Visa.

Vietnam

Of all four countries, Vietnam is the only country you cannot get a visa at a land-border post. For Vietnam, you have to get a visa beforehand at an embassy for land-border crossings. You can apply for a pre-approved visa online, if you fly into Hanoi or Saigon.

Vietnam visas are valid for 30 or 90 days, and can be single or multiple entry. The easiest way to get a Vietnam Tourist Visa is while still in Cambodia. Almost all large travel agencies and backpacker places will be able to help you out. At present, a one-month visa is $15 to $20, and a three-month visa is $25 to $45 (single, multi entry). There are also stamp duty fees, being $25 for single entry visas and $50 for multi entry visas. Processing normally takes five business days.

Note: Visas on arrival are not available for any border crossing, or any airport. You can get a pre-approve visa letter online, if you are flying into Saigon (Ho Chi Minh City), Da Nang, or Hanoi. You will use the letter to get your actual visa at the airport.

You cannot use the pre-approval letter to enter at any land-border crossings, as it is not an actual visa. There are many fraudulent websites claiming they can get a visa on arrival for you, and that it is valid for land border crossings. Only use the official government website. *https://vietnamvisa.govt.vn/*. You will need two color passport pictures, and pay the stamp fee in cash – US$ or VND.

Renewing Vietnam Visas

At the time of writing, you can extend your Vietnam visa for up to three months only once, while in Vietnam. That means, to stay long-term in Vietnam, you will need to leave Vietnam every six months. Tip - make your renewal a multi entry visa. Then, just before your visa expires, take a day trip to Cambodia, and back. A tour agency should be able to help you extend your visa again using the stamped Cambodia Visa. If you do not have a multi entry Vietnam visa, or wait until it expires, you will need to go to Phnom Penh or Siem Reap and wait a few days while you get another Vietnam visa.

Work visas are a bit harder to obtain than in Cambodia, and you will need a company to apply for you.

Laos

Laos Tourist Visas can easily be obtained at almost all border posts, even between Cambodia and Laos. However, know that this border post is plagued by corruption. Even with a Laos visa in hand, you will be expected to pay an exit stamp and entry stamp duty. This is bogus as no other Cambodian border charges exit stamp fees, but it cannot be avoided. The visa cost depends on the country you were born in, but is around $50 to $60.

Currently, getting a work visa in Laos is about the same as getting one in Vietnam, as in you will need a company to apply for you.

Renewing Laos Visas

Tourist Visas are valid for 30 days, and can be renewed for another 30 days while in Laos. Renewal is $2 a day, and is done at a Laos Immigration Office in most big cities such as Vientiane, or through travel agencies. As with Cambodia, after 60 days you will need to cross the border to get a new visa.

Thailand

You need a visa to enter Thailand, and will need to apply for it at a local embassy, or use a visa agency. . Two online companies you may try are *https://www.visahq.com* and *http://www.visaexpress.net/Thailand/thaitouristvisa.htm*. Tourist Visas are available from one to six months. At current, visas are from $65 to $200, depending on the length of the visa. If your home country is on the list of visa exempt countries, you can get an entry stamp that is valid for 30 days if arriving by air, and 15 days if arriving by land. The stamp is free, but you need to leave Thailand to renew your stamp.

As with Vietnam and Laos, it is a bit more difficult to get a Business Visa in Thailand than Cambodia. Your work will need to apply for you or try an online website. One I found, but did not use, is *http://www.visaexpress.net/Thailand/thaibusvisa.htm*.

Renewing Thai Visas

You can renew your visa once, while in Thailand, for 30 days. You cannot renew a visa exempt stamp and will need to leave Thailand and reenter it to get a new stamp. There is no limit on the amount of back-to-back visa border runs you can do. However, you are currently only allowed a maximum of 90 days in Thailand within a six-month period while using visa exempt stamps (although it is not always enforced).

Visas for visiting neighboring countries from Cambodia

If you are intending on spending some time in neighboring countries, such as Laos, Thailand and Vietnam, get your Visa in Cambodia before you depart for the neighboring country. Any large tour operator and most guesthouses, which deal with backpackers, will be able to arrange it for you. For Vietnam, definitely use this service, as you cannot get a visa on arrival for any Vietnam border crossing.

In Phnom Penh, I used Okay guesthouse for my Vietnam visa and would highly recommend staying there and obtaining your visa through their service.
See *http://www.okay-guesthouse.com/*

Overstaying your visa

Overstaying a visa is not recommended. It can make getting a new visa more costly or impossible to get.
Cambodia: Fines are around $5 a day for the first month of overstay and around $6 a day after that.
Laos: Fine is $10 a day for an overstay.
Thailand: **Do not overstay in Thailand**. You can be fined up to 20 000 Baht, which is approximately US $450.
Vietnam: **Do not overstay in Vietnam**. For up to two days overstay, you are normally only fined a few dollars and can pay the fine at the airport. For more than two days, it becomes a problem, and you will need to go to an immigration office and explain yourself. Expect to pay $100 easily or more for 15 days overstay, and around $200 for 30 days. More than a month overstay can get you into deep trouble. If you do not pay the fine, you will not leave the airport. If you did overstay, go and see a company in Vietnam to help you out before heading to the airport.

Departure Tax

Be aware that there is a departure tax if you leave by air – they are about $25 US. Most of the time, the fee is included in your airplane ticket. For most land-border crossings, you may pay around $2 to $5 exit stamp fees, depending on the border.

Important Read

1: Bring at least $80 to the border. Some places (remote border posts, especially after 4:00 pm), may require additional fees, which will not be backed down from.

2: Agents at some border posts will add their own fee on top of the visa fee for handling the applications for you. Many people see this as scams, but you have to see it in their light. For a few dollars, they are providing a service for you by removing the guesswork of filling out forms and standing in lines. If you really want, you can save a few dollars and do it all yourself, but in most cases, the speed with which they get things done, is a bargain.

3: DO NOT give your passport to a local person, or a small shop, promising they have contacts and can get your renewal done for you. Only use consulates, large travel agencies, or big backpacker places. There are many scams going around, and many tourists have lost their passports to a person that vanished after they gave it to them. There is a market for foreign passports.

4: The first time you overstay a visa, you will be given a warning. The second time you overstay, you will be banned up to six months or forever, depending on the length you overstayed and the reason you gave.

Popular overland border crossings

Thailand – Aranyprathet / Poipet
Laos - Veun Kham / Dom Kralor (note your Laos visa on arrival is reported to NOT always being available at this crossing or inflated fees causing problems. Suggest doing this crossing through a travel agent). Vietnam – Bavet / Moc Bai (You will cross here if you take a bus to Saigon).

Chapter 5: What To Take

In all honestly, all you need is cash and your passport, everything else just makes your journey a bit easier. If you have to, you can buy everything you need on the go.

Tip: If you have never backpacked, select items for your travels that are durable and multipurpose. The longer you intend to backpack, the bigger difference it makes to buy quality items that can stand up to a lot of abuse, as well as serve multiple roles in order to save weight and luggage space. An example is a leather pants belt with a pin buckle against a webbing belt with a sliding buckle. A webbing belt can take more abuse and water before it rots and breaks, and a sliding belt buckle can easily be adjusted, especially when you use the belt to strap items to your backpack, compress clothes to make them fit, strap backpacks down on a bumpy Tuk Tuk ride, and more. Be creative.

The following items are suggestions based on what I found useful on my travels. I believe they will benefit you as well.

Mobile Alarm Clock

You only need to miss your bus or airplane once, to realize the value of a good travel alarm clock. Backpacking takes a lot out of you, and many times, you may need to get up in the early hours of the morning to catch a bus. After a late night out or sleepless nights from the all-night bar's noise next-door, you may not hear your cell phone's alarm. Go for a small, slim line model, requiring AA or AAA batteries, which can wake the dead. If you have a model that runs on watch batteries, know that you may struggle to find replacement batteries, so take a spare if you intend to backpack long-term.

Flask

A good-quality flask is an essential item for long-term backpacking and handy for short trips. With the Asian heat, the ice-cold water, or soda, you just bought, will most likely be hot before you can finish it – especially if you buy a 1.5L water bottle to save money. Having ice-cold water or hot coffee, at hand, on long bus rides (especially overnight) is a blessing.

Get a good quality double insulated, stainless steel one of around 750ml to 1L. I bought a nice one with an insulated sleeve for $15 in Cambodia. Stay away from those with inner glass linings, as one drop, and it is a mess. Note that single-walled flasks, commonly used on bicycles and by joggers (plastic or metal), are not good at keeping liquids cold for long, especially in Asia. Unless you use a double walled, insulated flask, it's better to leave your flask at home and use purchased bottled water.

A Travel Pen

A small travel pen is useful on longer backpacking trips. Crossing borders require endless forms to fill out, and they normally have no pens to borrow. I suggest a small travel pen with a closed refill, as open-ended pens (like the normal Bic), leak when they are exposed to heat.

Color Passport-Sized Photos

These small self-portraits come in handy for visas, visa renewals, long-term room rental, work permits, as well as driver's permits (driving license). I suggest you keep some with you: four pictures for short visits and eight for longer stays. Note that at some borders and visa renewal places, you may be fined $1 to $5 for not having a picture. Some airports have passport instamatic machines, but they do not always work.

A Smart Phone

A smart phone can be one of the best aids you can have while backpacking. The longer you intend on backpacking, the more useful it becomes. Personally, I recommend an iPhone and for travel I use an iPhone4. From personal experience of testing a number of phones, they are overall the best travel phones. I do not suggest you go out and buy the latest iPhone, no, rather get an older model and use the rest of the money on travel. The applications, ease of use, as well as robustness, stability, and user friendliness, make this phone an all-round winner. In addition, I have no affiliation with Apple, should you wonder.

A smart phone allows you to quickly and easily connect to the Internet, call home on Skype, or use multiple on and offline map applications (GPS Linked), which will help you get where you need to be. Booking hotel tickets while you are still on the bus can be cheaper than walking into a hotel. You can also track your expenses, keep notes of places you want to see, add new friends' contact information, as well as update your blog and diary. Yes, you can do a lot with a laptop or tablet, but a smart phone is just easier to carry and hide.

Whatever phone you get, put it in a case (waterproof recommended), and put a screen protector on it.

Multi-Port Charger
Recharging tablets and smart phones can be a hassle in some hostels and hotels. Often, a room will only have one or two plug outlets. Even if you have a plug point per bed, you still have the problem of charging all your devices in the short time you are in your room at night. I suggest you get a USB charger that can charge at least two to four devices at once. Do make sure that the output of the device is at least 1 ampere per channel for phones, and 2 amperes per channel for tablets; else, your device will take a long time to charge. The longer your travels, the more valuable a multi-port charger will become. Personally, I use an Anker 4 port USB charger.

External Battery Pack
Long bus rides, and extended hours of using your smart phone's camera and possibly 3G Internet or internal GPS, can leave you with a dead device before the day is over. Power failures are also common in Asia, especially in the rainy season.

If you intend on using your phone to take pictures, retrieve email, use the internal GPS for maps, or do the same with a tablet, I suggest you get an external battery pack. They have come a long way in design, and you have a multitude of options. Good things to look for are battery packs that are not dedicated to a specific device, but have USB ports. A battery pack that can charge two devices at the same time is a bonus.

For phones, you are looking for a device that can put out a minimum of 500milli amp to 1 amp, and for tablets you are looking for an output of at least 1 amp to 2 amps. To charge only a cellphone, I would suggest nothing smaller than 5000mAh, and for tablets, I suggest at least 10 000mAh. The more remote, and longer bus or motorcycle rides you do, the more battery power you will need. Personally, I have two Anker 15 000mAh battery packs.

Small Flashlight

When backpacking in Asia, you will eventually have the need for a flashlight. They are handy when searching for something, packing your stuff in a hostel while everyone is still asleep, walking or cycling back home from a night out, or hiking to your bus pick up early in the morning. Not to mention possible power outages and going into caves or searching deeper into temples.

If you are only going for a few days, then you may be okay with the light most smart phones can provide. However, for a week or longer backpacking experience, I suggest a small, handheld light such as the LED version Solitaire from Maglite, or something similar. At 37 lumens, the Maglite is powerful enough to walk at night if you need to, while being small enough to fit on a key chain. This comes in very handy if you take night buses. They often stop at dimly lit places for you to use the restroom and buy snacks. Forget about the cheap nine or more LED lights – they are bulky and do not give off enough light. Get a small one that takes AA or AAA batteries, and has a Cree LED light and gives at least 30 Lumens.

If you intend on backpacking for longer duration, I suggest getting an additional headlight with at least 80 or 100 lumens, such as the Black Diamond Storm headlight. Unless you are thinking of going into caves or motorcycling in the bush at night, you really do not need the added weight of a bigger flashlight with a gazillion lumens. With 100 lumens, you can easily light up a room during power failures, while giving good battery life for walking to a taxi, bus, or even hotel at odd hours of the night. Remember, what use is a light, as powerful as the sun, if it only lasts 30 to 60 minutes?

Look for a light that takes AA or AAA batteries, and not watch or RC123 batteries. I would also avoid internal rechargeable batteries. Anything other than AA and AAA batteries are not easy to come by, and with internal rechargeable batteries you may not get the chance to charge the unit. It may also require you to carry an additional adapter or charger. Large handheld flashlights are too heavy for backpacking and getting C and D-cell batteries are sometimes a problem.

A Fleece Top With a Hoody

Although you are going to SE Asia, where it is mostly warm and tropical, it can get cold in the rainy season. You may also find that many tour buses run the air conditioner flat out, making a warm item very handy. Fleece jackets are lightweight for the warmth they provide, and compress and pack very easily.

Rolled up, the jacket is also functional as a pillow when you are taking long rides or need to wait for an airplane or bus. Please note that the morning air can get chilly as you head out to see the sun rise over Angkor Wat or some other far-out temple.

A Small Lock

Hostels often have lockable storage spaces under the beds or in cupboards where you can keep your belongings. However, few places supply locks. There have also been cases where hostel workers make spare keys for the locks and then rob the customers, and then denied having any spare keys.

You may also consider getting a lock with an integrated steel cable, or get a bicycle seat lock cable. This will allow you to lock backpacks together, and lock your backpack to your bed or clothes railing, should there be no lockable cupboard to store your belongings.

White Gold

In Asia, especially Cambodia, it is not a question of will you get an upset stomach, but when. The longer you backpack, the higher your chances. And as always, you will get sick when the roadside toilets have no toilet paper. In fact, few roadside toilets on bus routes have toilet paper, as toilet paper is not normally used outside large cities, but rather they have a bucket of water.

You might also come to a hotel or hostel late at night, and find that someone used up the last toilet paper. I always carry a full roll of toilet paper with me. You can remove the inner cardboard cylinder and press the roll together to save space.

Tube of Sanitizer

Hand sanitizer comes in small bottles that are easy to pack. Often, you will find no washbasin to wash your hands after using the hole in the ground, or tree that serves as a toilet. Not washing your hands before eating, especially after using the toilet, is a good way to ensure getting very ill.

Good Earplugs and Eye Shields

If you backpack for a while, you will have to deal with short-term backpackers who love to party late and come back drunk at 4am in the morning, or want to sit and chat with the lights on until the sun comes up. If that does not get you, then the dripping showerhead, barking street dogs, or all-night disco next door will. In addition, just as you finally fall asleep, the monks will start chanting over a loudspeaker at 5am, not to mention the 7-day wailing when someone dies, or the 4 to 7-day street party for weddings, all done over a loudspeaker. It is kind of an ego thing to be able to afford the biggest and loudest amplifiers, especially in Cambodia. They also enjoy hiring professional wailers for funerals and professional all night disco jocks for weddings. Earplugs also help for long bus rides, and boring airport transfers. Good ones are the sponge, reusable earplugs or the silicon balls often found in drug stores (pharmacy). The silicon balls block more sound.

Sports Towel

In most hostels and all hotels, you will get a towel. Thus, unless you go for the $1 to $3 a day option, you can leave your towel at home. However, if you are backpacking for a month, or more, and plan to visit a few hostels, consider getting a sport's towel (micro fiber towel). They are very light to pack, dry very fast, and can serve as a pillow when rolled up. Do get one that is of decent size, preferably the same size as a normal towel.

Tampons and Pads

In major cities such as Bangkok, Siem Reap, Phnom Penh, Saigon and Hanoi, it is not too difficult to find tampons and pads. However, not all brands are sold even if you do find any, and in the countryside and smaller towns, you may struggle to find any at all. I would recommend you bring enough to last your trip.

Chapter 6: What To Leave at Home

The following items you can strongly consider leaving at home. Although some have their use, the added weight and packing space they require will not justify taking them along, especially on shorter trips. Where an item is useful for long-term backpacking, it will be mentioned.

Umbrella and Rain Jacket

Forget about an umbrella, most of the time it will just blow away in the wind or get damaged. Rain jackets take too much space, are heavy, and do not cover your backpacks. It's better to get a cheap poncho for 50 cents, keeping in mind the rain covers you get for backpacks are good for only light rain. Eventfully the shoulder straps get soaked, and it moves down into the backpack. Water also runs between your back and the backpack, eventually soaking through. Put a poncho over you and the backpack.

Rechargeable Batteries

Changing the batteries in your flashlight, or most other devices for rechargeable batteries, seems like a good idea. However, most AAA and AA rechargeable batteries do not hold the same power as good-quality alkaline batteries. Rechargeable batteries also do not seem to hold their charge for long periods when not used. AA and AAA batteries are readily available, so if you need to save weight, you can buy a supply when you get to your hotel.

Unless you are going to backpack for a few months or will be using the device a lot (bicycling home at night), you are better off using non-rechargeable batteries. Even on long backpacking trips the batteries in a good-quality Cree LED flashlight should last multiple bus rides. Remember a charger for rechargeable batteries takes up space, and if the batteries are not used constantly they deteriorate to the point where they will refuse to take a charge.

Mosquito Net

I have to admit I read in a book not to bother with a mosquito net before I went to Siem Reap, and still took one. It was a mistake. I used the net for two nights, and had to throw it away as it was covered in bed bugs. From then on, after changing hotels, I traveled all over Cambodia, Laos, Thailand, and Vietnam, and never needed one again.

Many places have mosquito nets, while others have screen-covered windows. The best I found was burning mosquito coils and putting an electric, mosquito-poison vaporizer in the room. Do use insect deterrents such as Deet or citronella containing products.

Water Purifying Device and Tablets

I had an expensive UV-light water purifier, and never used it. The drinking water you get at restaurants and hostels in all four countries is bottled water. Although you can drink the tap water in large cities, most people do not, especially in Cambodia. Even locals in small villages drink bottled water, unless they have a stream nearby or use ground water, however, restaurants still supply bottled water – just make sure the bottle is still sealed.

Hat

The sun in SE Asia is relentless, but you do need a hat when going outside. Yet, hats are so cheap and the options so plentiful, that you can easily get one when you arrive. The hat will then be a souvenir of your adventure when you go home.

Fancy Stuff

Taking expensive jewelry or prized possessions, such as a zippo lighter your grandfather gave you, on a backpacking trip is a good way to lose it. Backpacking can be fast paced, as you rush out of your room before the sun is up, to see attractions or to catch a ride. You can easily forget something in your room, not to mention backpackers that think it is their right to relieve you of your expensive items for their benefit. If you are not prepared to lose it, it's better to leave it at home, especially on longer backpacking trips, or if you are staying in multiple dorm rooms. This advice goes for fancy clothes as well.

12v Car Charger and Adaptors

Buses do not have charge points for each seat (except some overnight buses that have USB ports), and forget about using the minibus's plug point, as the driver is using it for his plethora of phones. If you need to charge your devices on the go, you are better off with a good-quality external battery pack.

Multi Tool

You may feel like Rambo; however, there are few needs for a multi tool on short backpacking trips. The small keychain ones are handy now and again, but not really worth buying just for your trip. Even on long backpacking trips, you hardly ever need them; as well they are easily stolen, weigh a lot, and are expensive. Considering that, a night in a hostel is around $5, yet a good-quality tool can be $50 to $100+, which is a lot of vacation money for something you are probably going to lose or never use.

Laptop

Taking your laptop to Skype with friends, update your blog posts, or read books sounds like a good idea. However, almost all hostels have a computer you can use, and a smart phone can be used to stay in contact and access your email. Laptops do not like backpacking, and they are a target for crime. If you are going for a longer duration and want to take a laptop, make sure you take a good-quality laptop lock cable with. If you have a tablet, it may serve you better in the long run, rather than a laptop.

Sunscreen and Insect Repellent

Bring only a small amount of each for immediate use, as you can buy these items in most shops. The added weight and space they take up, with the risk of a bottle opening and messing up your clothes, does not warrant bringing large amounts.

Neck Pillow

Unless yours is inflatable, consider using a rolled up fleece jacket instead. The once or twice you may use the pillow, compared to the storage space it takes up, does not warrant bringing one along, unless you can deflate and fold it away.

Chapter 7: Bag Selection

Bag selection is a very personal choice, and ultimately you have to carry it and live with it. The following are only suggestions, based on what I found to work, both for me and other backpackers I met on the road. I've also included some things that did not work well. I know there are backpackers who travel with only a toothbrush, but to me that is not backpacking, that is bumming it. Likewise, I am not one for being a barfly, spending my days recovering and nights drinking in different bars. Backpacking for me is getting out and experiencing life and meeting local people. For this, you need more than a toothbrush and a stale T-shirt.

For backpacking in Asia, try to avoid hard suitcases and hiking backpacks with solid outside frames. The solid frames make it harder to load on a tuk tuk or under a minivan's seat. It is also hard to hold onto a suitcase while you cling for dear life on the back of a motorcycle taxi.

Hard suitcases are, in most cases, not any more secure than a backpack, as clasps can easily be opened and resealed. Many suitcase locks can easily be picked. Suitcases and hiking backpacks may not fit in backpack storage spaces at hostels, and are a pain on a train.

The size of the backpack depends entirely on what comfort, and luxury items, you plan to take along. However, regardless of how long you plan to travel, I suggest you get a small (around 24L) backpack or a laptop bag. Always pack your most important items in this bag; such as your laptop, phone, tablet, wallet, passport and so on. Never put this bag in a cargo hold of an airplane or bus, but always keep it with you. I would also suggest you carry a change of underwear in the small backpack on long journeys, where you will not have access to your main backpack.

A Few Days to a Week Backpacking

For a few days to two weeks, I suggest a 55 to 65L backpack. Most of these can fit in an overhead compartment of an airplane or under a minivan taxi's seat. You should easily be able to carry enough clothes for a week, and wash them as you travel. This will make you very mobile, and free you from the worry of lost luggage, if you take the backpack with you on airplanes, trains and buses.

A Month to Two Months

If you plan on backpacking for a month or two, I suggest a 70 to 90L backpack. This is what most short-term backpackers go with. It makes you very mobile, while having most of what you will need with you. Add to this your day bag or small backpack as suggested before.

Long-Term Backpacking

For long-term backpacking, I suggest a 90L to 110L main backpack, with a 55 to 65L secondary backpack, as well as the small day bag mentioned earlier. Although you will be slightly less mobile compared to having one large backpack, I've found on long backpacking travels one tends to stay longer in one spot. In addition, having the extra personal items with you will help you to stay focused on your dreams. Long-term backpacking can be hard, and a little bit of comfort can go a long way.

Personally, I have a 70L Eagle Creek main backpack, with a zip on day bag of 24L. However, I am against removable day bags, as I have seen how it hampers me. The 94L backpack is reduced to a 70L, but you cannot put the day bag, with the main backpack, in a cargo hold, as it contains your laptop and other valuables. Personally, I recommend getting a single large backpack, and then purchase an additional separate small backpack. That extra 24L makes a big difference in the end.

I recommend not going for the standard top load backpacks with a flap going over. Backpacks in general are not that secure, and these are even worse as they cannot actually lock. I suggest a backpack that has a zipper that totally closes and is front-loading. This way, you can lay the backpack flat and open it up like a suitcase – items are easier reached. Know that smaller items tend to work their way to the bottom of your bag, making them hard to reach with a top load backpack.

Regardless of the backpack you select, I recommend making sure it has a hip belt. The belt helps to relieve the weight on your shoulders. Even a day backpack containing 2L of water starts to dig into your shoulders at the end of the day. A hip belt will also help prevent the backpack from moving around, as you cycle though rice paddies or blast through Vietnam's mountains on a motorcycle.

Do note that no backpack is safe from theft, as zippers can be broken and the bag itself cut open. However, for long-term backpacking, the solid suitcases are more of a nuisance than the added security they provide.

Get backpack covers or put your bag in a black trash bag when putting it in the cargo hold of buses, especially in Cambodia and between Phnom Penh and Siem Reap. The amount of dust that can pile onto or into your backpack is amazing. In the rainy season, your backpack may become soaked or covered in mud, especially on cheap buses.

Chapter 8: Immunization

There are a number of different immunization shots that are highly recommended before you travel to Asia. Remember, it is cheaper to get a shot, than be treated for something – even if you can find or get proper treatment. Here is a short-list, but do talk to your local doctor or immunization center long before you want to travel. Furthermore, know that in some cases, shots may need to be ordered or cannot be found (I had a problem getting shots in the Cayman Islands), and in some cases you may need to get a doctor's prescription for some. (When I left Cayman, I went to the USA for two weeks before going to Cambodia. I needed to see a doctor to get a prescription for a shot before I was allowed to get it. It added $100 to the bill.)

Hepatitis A

Hepatitis A is an acute infectious disease that affects the liver, and you may not show any symptoms, especially if you're young and healthy. Symptoms normally show two to six weeks after infection and lasts normally around eight weeks. Symptoms include nausea, vomiting, diarrhea, yellow skin, fever, and abdominal pain. You can have recurring symptoms up to about six months after your initial infection. If untreated and you have a weak immune system, or already damaged liver, it can lead to acute liver failure.

Hepatitis A is a major threat in SE Asia, especially Cambodia. The disease is usually spread by eating food, or drinking water, contaminated with infected feces (the result of servers not washing their hands properly). Other means of spreading are through shellfish that have not been cooked properly, or have had close contact with an infectious person.

You will need a blood test to confirm the infection.
There is no specific treatment beyond rest and medications for nausea or diarrhea, as recommended and needed. Be aware the disease can reoccur for life. The infection normally resolves on its own; but the only treatment for acute liver failure is a costly liver transplant.

Hepatitis B

Like Hepatitis A, Hepatitis B is an infectious illness that affects the liver. However, this one is a bit more of a problem as it causes liver inflammation, vomiting, jaundice, and in some cases death. The disease responds poorly to current medication, and chronic Hepatitis B may eventually cause cirrhosis and liver cancer.

The virus is transmitted by exposure to infectious body fluids, such as blood, semen, and vaginal fluids. However, viral DNA has been detected in saliva, tears, and urine of chronic carriers. The disease can also be spread to an unborn baby if the mother is infected. You can also become infected by blood transfusions, dialysis, sharing razors or toothbrushes with an infected person, or from non-sterilized tattoo needles, and of course, sharing needles when doing drugs.

Note that the Hepatitis B virus is 50 to 100 times more infectious than HIV and about a third of the world's population has been infected at one point in their lives, with an estimated 350 million who are chronic carriers.

Symptoms include loss of appetite, nausea, vomiting, body aches, mild fever, and dark urine, which eventually progresses to develop jaundice. The illness lasts for a few weeks and then gradually improves in most affected people. A few people may get severe liver disease (fulminant hepatic failure), and may die as a result. The infection may also be entirely symptomless and go unrecognized, which can lead to cirrhosis and liver cancer, over a period of several years.

A serum or blood test is needed to confirm infection.

The infection does not normally require treatment and clears up spontaneously. Chronic infection needs treatment, and is treated over a period of six months to a year. However, do note that none of the available drugs can clear the infection; all they can do is hopefully stop the virus from replicating and minimizing liver damage.

Japanese Encephalitis

Japanese encephalitis (Japanese B encephalitis) is a disease caused by the mosquito-borne Japanese encephalitis virus. Pigs and wild birds (herons) are reservoirs of the virus. Incubation is around 5 to 15 days after infection, with the vast majority of infections being asymptomatic. The good news is that only about 1 in 250 infections develop into encephalitis. However, when it does, severe rigors occur. Fever, headache, and malaise are non-specific symptoms that may last from one to six days. It can worsen to neck rigidity, cachexia, hemiparesis, convulsions, high fever, mental retardation, coma and death.

Lifelong neurological defects such as deafness, emotional liability and hemiparesis have been noted.

There is no specific treatment for Japanese encephalitis. Treatment is supportive in nature; being fed, and breathing or seizure control as required. The disease is not transmitted from person to person.

Malaria

Malaria remains a big problem outside of the main city of Phnom Penh in Cambodia, and Bangkok in Thailand.

There is no immunization for malaria. However, there is medication available to help prevent it if you are bitten. The problem remains that the malaria strains have become more and more resistant to drugs. This is especially the case in Battambang, Cambodia. The best option would be to take medication as suggested by known experts, and to minimize being bitten. You can readily get mosquito repellant in most shops, including non-Deet containing lotions and sprays. Mosquito coils and electric diffusers are also readily available for use in your room. Also consider mosquito nets. Although hot, try to wear long-sleeve shirts and long trousers with shoes. If using a Deet containing product, try to get one that contains 12% or more Deet, or reapply every hour as the Deet evaporates over time. When sleeping, wear socks to help prevent pesky ankle biters. A ceiling fan helps, as the mosquitoes have weak wings, and they will also struggle to find your body heat and CO_2 trail.

A blood test is needed to confirm infection. There are a number of different strains of malaria, which require different medications. However, as noted, Battambang has a very high medication resistant strain.

The signs and symptoms normally begin 8 to 25 days following infection. Symptoms include flu-like symptoms and may include headache, fever, shivering, joint pain, vomiting, hemolytic anemia, jaundice, retinal damage, convulsions, and hemoglobin in the urine. However, the classic symptom of malaria is paroxysm (a cyclical occurrence of sudden coldness followed by shivering and then fever and sweating). It normally occurs every two or three days, but sometimes less. Severe malaria can lead to seizures and coma. Symptoms can reoccur from 8 to 24 weeks if the infection is not cleared totally.

Malaria is treated with antimalarial medications, depending on the type and severity of the disease, and patients usually do not need hospitalization. Resolution would depend on the type and severity of the disease.

Know that resistance to Artemisinin (main form of malaria treatment with piperaquine) has been found in Cambodia and Vietnam. Mefloquine (Lariam) is an alternative option and is effective in most areas of Vietnam, except the Mekong Delta region, where resistance to the drug occurs. Do consult a doctor before taking any medication. For more information, , see *http://www.cdc.gov/malaria/map/index.html* and *http://www.malaria.com/overview/malaria-countries-map*.

Rabies

Rabies is a viral disease that causes acute inflammation of the brain. Symptoms usually occur one to three months after contracting the disease, but can occur in less than one week to more than a year after infection. It all depends on how far the virus needs to travel to reach the central nervous system.

Early symptoms may include fever, headache and tingling at the site of exposure. Violent movements, uncontrolled excitement, fear of water, inability to move parts of the body, confusion, and unconsciousness can occur. Once symptoms appear, it almost always results in death.

The most common method of infection is by a bite or scratch from an animal (or human). Dogs, followed by bats, are the most common animals that infect humans: with rodents very seldom causing infection. Rabies vaccine and sometimes rabies immunoglobulin are effective in preventing the disease if given before the start of symptoms. Washing wounds for 15 minutes with soap and water have been reported to be somewhat effective. Few people survive rabies infection even with extensive treatment, and it is reported that up to 55 000 people die every year from rabies. Prevention is key.

Southeast Asia, especially Cambodia, have many stray dogs and the risk of being bitten is real, especially in smaller villages or if you walk to the outer edges of town. Be aware that people do live in the Angkor grounds, along some of the farther ruins, and they have dogs that run wild. Dogs attacked me on a few occasions while visiting some of the outer temples. I only managed to escape because I was on a motorcycle. Do be careful when visiting the outer temples.

Tetanus

Tetanus is a medical condition with prolonged contraction of the skeletal muscles. Infection normally occurs through wound contamination, as the infection progresses, muscles spasm and lock the jaw and other muscles of the body. Be careful with open wounds.

Symptoms normally begin with mild spasms of the jaw muscles and can affect the chest, neck, back, abdominal, and buttocks muscles. Other symptoms include drooling, excessive sweating, fever, hand or foot spasms, irritability, swallowing difficulty, and uncontrolled urination or defecation. Death can occur. The incubation period is normally eight days, but can be a few months.

Tetanus is caused by the tetanus bacterium, Clostridium tetani, and is often associated with rust, especially rusty nails. However, anything that accumulates rust can harbor the bacteria. Know that it is not the rust, but the bacteria's love for rough surfaces that attracts it. Thus any rough surface could have the bacteria, and an already open wound can be infected. However, the bacteria can also reside in heroin, and injection users are at a high risk of contracting the bacteria.

In mild cases treatment requires drugs, but more severe cases will require hospitalization in intensive care, and possibly mechanical ventilation (could be on a ventilator for up to a month).

In order to survive a tetanus infection, breathing and proper nutrition are required: 3,500 to 4,000 calories with at least 150 g of protein per day is needed. It is often given in liquid form through a tube directly into the stomach, or through an IV route. Full recovery normally takes four to six weeks while the body regenerates destroyed nerve axon terminals.

Typhoid

Typhoid fever is a bacterial disease transmitted by the ingestion of food or water contaminated with bacterium Salmonella enterica. It is generally acquired through indirect contact with fecal matter of an infected person. Due to people in SE Asia often not washing their hands after defecating, including poor hygiene for working with fish products, Typhoid is a real concern, especially in smaller towns and villages.

Early symptoms, normally in the first week, include fever fluctuations, malaise, headache, and cough. A bloody nose and abdominal pain can also occur. Later symptoms are a high fever, bradycardia, and delirium. Rose spots can also appear on the lower chest and abdomen, as well as internal bleeding can occur. Normally at the end of the third week, the fever goes down.

With treatment, Typhoid is normally not fatal, and symptoms last for up to a month. Untreated, up to 30% death rate is reported.

Chapter 9: Health

Although medical service is not at the peak of world standards in most of SE Asia, it is getting remarkably better. Medicine and services are, however, very cheap, and a number of western doctors and dentist are coming to put up shop. Thus, you can get good service at a fraction of the price you would have paid at home. This is especially true for dental work in Cambodia. However, for life-threatening illnesses, or operations, you may need to be flown to Hong Kong or Bangkok, especially if you are in the countryside.

Things To Know

Know that people sometimes get a commission if they call an ambulance for you. It can be as high as $50, and it will be included in your bill. Although drugs may be cheap, going to a hospital or clinic may not be. An IV costs $10 on average and the cost of a visit to a clinic can easily exceed $100, and that's only for using their bed. Doctors sometimes give out medicine without any tests (especially in Cambodia), thus you may not get what you need, or you may be allergic.

What Is 911?

In most of SE Asia, there is no central service where you dial one number and it is linked to the police, ambulance, and fire service. You need to call each one individually. The services do not have the means to easily communicate with each other. Meaning, even if a police officer is at the scene, he / she cannot just radio dispatch and request an ambulance for you – they have to call as well. Emergency evacuation is not on the same standard as in America or the UK. If you are seriously injured, there is no easily available helicopter to evacuate you.

A large number of backpackers are injured from falling off a motorcycle, or burning themselves against a hot exhaust pipe. Most of the time, the backpacker was intoxicated or stoned when the accident occurred.

Cuts

Due to the tropic environment, cuts, like bedbug and mosquito bites that you scratch open, can become infected and lead to serious problems. For minor cuts or any open wounds, go to a local pharmacy and get ointment, and a Band-Aid (plaster). If you are planning on backpacking for a month or more, I suggest you bring a small tube of Neosporin, or better still Brave Soldier if you can get it, plus a small number of Band-Aids.

Washing Hands

Washing your hands is key to staying healthy, and many Asians do not, and they touch things you will later touch. Do note, however, that even in many public toilets, you may not find soap. So, bring a small bottle of hand soap with you, especially if you plan to stay in rural towns or travel a lot on cheaper bus services.

Doctors

For emergencies, if you need to see a doctor, your best bet is to go to a hospital or a clinic. For non-emergencies, you may ask Facebook groups what the best private doctors are at that moment, and where they are located – just type in the place that you are at in Facebook. Such as Siem Reap, or Bangkok, and look for community groups.

Dengue Fever

Dengue fever (also called joint breaking fever) is more of a problem in the cities than Malaria. Mosquitoes spread the disease. Be aware that the "tiger mosquito" or "moo kham" bites in the daytime. This mosquito is larger than the average ones found there, and has a striped abdomen. Mosquitoes breed in water, so be more aware in the rainy season, or around hotels and guesthouses with ponds and lots of potted plants. Some places use a chemical called "abate" that kills the larvae in the water – ask the hotel if they use it.

Symptoms usually begin four to six days after infection and can last for up to 10 days. Symptoms may include high fever, severe headaches, pain behind the eyes, joint and muscle pain, nausea, vomiting, skin rash, nosebleeds, bleeding gums, and easy bruising. The symptoms may progress to massive bleeding, shock, and death. This is called dengue shock syndrome (DSS).

People with weakened immune systems, as well as those with a second or subsequent dengue infection are believed to be at greater risk for developing dengue hemorrhagic fever. A blood test is needed to confirm and treat Dengue Fever.

There is no specific medicine to treat dengue infection, and treatment is normally no more than painkillers with acetaminophen. Avoid medicines with aspirin, which could worsen the bleeding. Rest, drink plenty of fluids, and see your doctor. If you start to feel worse in the first 24 hours after your fever goes down, you should get to a hospital immediately to be checked for complications.

Dehydration
SE Asia has a year round relatively hot climate. Know that you may sweat a lot more than you think, and can easily get dehydrated and pass out without warning.

Sunstroke is a big problem, therefore wear a hat and drink plenty of water. Note that drinks containing alcohol and caffeine will cause you to urinate more and further dehydrate you. Water is sold all over in bottled form; try to stay away from local tap water. It is advised that you constantly take sips of water as you walk, and drink at least 1.5L of water a day.

Dehydration can lead to headaches, a general feeling of un-wellness, as well as placing extra stress on your heart. This is a significant concern for people with heart or blood pressure troubles.

If you start to get dizzy from heat stroke, pour some water over your head and neck, wet a T-shirt or cloth in cold water and put that on your head and neck. Drink cold water, and get to shade to rest. You may want to return to your hotel if you have an air-conditioning unit or a shop or mall that has air-conditioning.

Food Poisoning

Food poisoning is one of the leading illnesses that travelers experience…and not just in developing countries. Realize that there are always bacteria and germs around, and in your country you are used to them, but there will be germs and bacteria that are foreign to your immune system, especially if you have not traveled much in your life.

People touch things, and then you touch it as well. It is impossible to avoid coming in contact with new germs and bacteria. However, washing your hands before you eat (wet wipes may be needed), and after you have gone to the toilet, will greatly reduce your risk of getting sick.

Apart from being clean yourself, watching where and what you eat can greatly reduce the risk of getting sick, however, realize that the longer you stay in Asia, the greater the risk is of getting sick. The first two months after arriving in Cambodia, I loved my toilet. There were times when I stayed almost a week mostly in my room.

Although you are not likely to get sick in a week's stay if eating in hotels and restaurant, but you may get sick if eating at roadside places or at the temple ruins. It is not that the food is different, but that it may not have been cooked properly. Chicken, fish and pork can be a problem so select beef.

If you have a sensitive stomach, take food (bananas or a food hamper from your hotel) with when you go out exploring temples or other attractions. Remember, if it is not cooked, fried or peeled, avoid it if you have a sensitive stomach. And keep to bottled water and avoid eating meat in local markets. The meat is often cut up on wooden blocks that rarely are washed with soap, if they are washed at all – bits of food stay in the wooden grooves and is heaven for bacteria. If you get sick, head to a local pharmacy, and immediately get some medication for it, as it will get worse and spoil a few days of your trip. Also drink plenty of water or sports drinks (PowerAde or Gatorade) while you are sick, as you will dehydrate.

Note: always wipe off the water that is around the rim of soda or beer cans when you purchase them from places that keep them iced in red coolers. That ice water is not that clean. In fact, it is best if you wipe off all cans that you purchase, and use a straw.

Try to avoid canned fruit drinks sold in the countryside, even if they are stored in red cooler boxes, especially in Cambodia. Often the drinks have been repeatedly heated and cooled and can cause problems. I had a few nasty surprises.

Ice Blocks

Unless you are in a far-out village and are unlucky, the ice that you get in your drinks comes from a factory and is clean. The ice blocks you see locals cut up on the back of a truck are only used to keep items cool and not normally used in drinks. If the ice in your drink is crushed and you are not in a respectable restaurant, be a bit wary. However, ice that is cubed or in cylinders, with holes, is fine.

Toilets on Bus Routes

Only upper class bus tours have toilets on board, and they do not always work. Most trains have good toilets, especially in Thailand and Vietnam (at the time of this writing, Cambodia's public train service was still not running). Tour buses stop at roadside restaurants; however, the restaurants and toilet status is normally on par with the price you paid for your bus ticket. You may also be asked to either buy food from the restaurant or pay a fee before you are allowed to use the toilet. Always carry at least $1 (local currency suggested) with you on bus tours, even if you are leaving the country.

If you are lucky enough to get an actual toilet and not a hole in the ground, lift the seat of the toilet before you sit down. Check for cockroaches, spiders, and the occasional snake, especially in remote villages or backpacker places. Also, sanitize the seat of the toilet with a wet wipe or hand sanitizer and toilet paper before you sit down. On trains, the toilet is often just a hole in the train's floor – try to avoid using the toilet when the train is in the station.

Medication

You can get a range of medication or alternatives in SE Asia in large towns. Many pharmacies do not require a prescription for schedule drugs, especially in Cambodia. This has led to a misuse of drugs.

Do be aware that the pharmacy does not always provide the medication's box or information pamphlet, especially if you buy only half the box. You may also find that the staff is not be medically trained. Asking a cashier at a pharmacy for advice may be riskier than doing a Google search for suggested medication for your symptoms. Remember that many Asians will not easily say they do not know, but will save face and smile while they lie to you, trying to avoid an argument or embarrassing situation. I know it does not always make sense to lie to avoid an argument, but that is how it is. And for the most part, they will not see you again, so hence they have no argument or embarrassing situation with you.

In Thailand and Vietnam, most pharmacies are good. In Cambodia, U care is the better option. In Laos, take what you get.

Vegetarians and People Allergic to Fish Take Note

Traditional Cambodian food is often spiced with Prahok. This gives the food a salty, pungent taste, and is a paste that is made from fermented fish (usually of mud fish). This is even put into vegetarian dishes, and in almost all soups. Be aware it is fish (if you are vegetarian or allergic to fish), but also Prahok needs to be cooked or fried properly, and if not can make you very ill. Know that raw Prahok cannot be stored very long, and in smaller villages, it may have been cooked some time ago to preserve it.

If Prahok is not used, shrimp paste (made from fermented ground shrimp mixed with salt) is often substituted. This is a common ingredient in dips for fish or vegetables, and may be a bigger problem for people allergic to shellfish. When in doubt, order European dishes and not traditional dishes. The Prahok normally shows as oily drops in vegetable soup.

When Traveling on Rivers

If you go out on a boat, especially to the floating villages in Thailand, wear a mouth mask. You can get cheap throwaway ones, or buy an expensive material one. This is the same, as you will see many locals use for the dust. Because the water around the floating villages is used as toilets and sewerage dumps, there are loads of bacteria in the water. Only one drop on your lips, accidentally licked up, is enough to give you worms or many other illnesses. See a pharmacy or doctor immediately if you start to feel ill a day or so after a boat ride.

Swimming

Do not swim in rivers or streams unless it has running water. Watch out for hidden dangers such as left over jetty supports or rubbish that was dumbed in the water. Be careful if you have a cut or get cut, as bacteria can easily enter the site. Clean all open wounds with sterile water and then treat with an antibacterial cream and dress the wound. If the wound is large or starts to worsen, go see a doctor immediately.

Be careful when swimming in the ocean, especially in Thailand. Raw, untreated sewage is often pumped directly into the ocean, just off a beach. You run the risk of getting infections, such as Hep A and C.

Chapter 10: Money Matters

Money is what makes the world, and your adventures go around. Following is advice on how to pay for your expenses.

Cash

In all four countries, cash is king. However, only in Cambodia is the US dollar widely accepted. In fact, it is the preferred method of payment in Cambodia. In all four countries, EURO and POUND are not accepted by street vendors and small shops, and by very few large restaurants and hotels. You are better of exchanging it to local money or US$.

In Cambodia, the local money is Riel. However, as mentioned already, US$ is the preferred currency for payment for almost all transactions, except for smaller items in markets, such as a bunch of bananas (50c to $1). However, paying with a $5 note, or less, for small items is normally not a problem.
1 US$ is roughly 4000 Riel in the streets for Cambodia.
ATM machines dispense US$ currency only, unless you have a Cambodian bank account.

In Thailand, Baht is used by street vendors and smaller restaurants, and only larger shops accept US$, even in Bangkok. No one wanted to take US$ on the street, and I ended up exchanging US$ to Baht at my hostel, as they gave me a better rate than the money exchangers. Riel is accepted by many roadside shops at the Poipet border in Thailand, but no further inland.
1 US$ is roughly 32 Baht on the street.
ATM machines dispense Baht currency only.

In Laos, except for major tourist towns, Kip (LAK) is the method of payment. As I made my way through Laos, from the bottom to Vientiane, I could not even pay for a tuk tuk ride in Pakse (a large town) that was about US$2, with a US$10 note, even when I told the driver he could keep the change. I had to exchange money at a nearby hotel to pay the tuk tuk. Yet, in Vientiane I could pay small roadside restaurants with US$, as long as the bills I gave came close to the money owed. Change was given back in local Kip. I also had no problem exchanging US$ at my hostel to local Kip, or pay for my room and food at the hostel in US$.

1 US$ is roughly 8000 Kip on the street.

ATM machines dispense Kip currency only.

In Vietnam, Vietnamese dong (VND) is the method of payment outside larger cities. Inside larger cities, such as Saigon, Hanoi and Hoi An, I had no problem paying at most places with US$. Some street vendors, and smaller restaurants, did accept US$ in larger cities, but only when the bills I gave was close to the bill owed. In the mountains and away from the tourist towns, VND was all that was accepted, and I could not even exchange US$ to VND at the hotels where I stayed. If you are doing countryside trips, take enough VND with until you come to a larger town.

1 US$ is roughly 21 000VND in the street.

ATM machines dispense VND currency only.

Credit and Debit Cards

In all four countries, Amex cards seem to be a problem. Some shops accept Amex cards, but most do not. You are better off with cash than trying to pay by Amex.

Larger hotels, restaurants, and guesthouses readily accept visa and Master Cards, however, only if the amount exceeds about US$20. Roadside stalls, small shops, and most hostels, do not have the facility to accept cards. I have a Visa and a Master Card, and suggest having both for longer travels. If not possible, Visa seems to be the more accepted card, but I have yet to have a problem with Master Card.

Many shops add approximately 3 to 5% to the bill, if paying by card, therefore, if you are paying for expensive items, such as shopping in Bangkok, or paying for your room, you may be better off drawing money at an ATM (automatic teller machine) and paying in cash (normally amounts of around $150 to $200). It is normally cheaper to draw a large amount (around $500 or more), and then pay cash for small items, rather than paying service charge fees on every small purchase with a card.

Drawing Money

Almost every town and city in all four countries have ATM machines, except for small rural villages. However, do not rely on it, as they run dry of money when loads of tourists descend on them. Always have some backup money.

When drawing from an ATM, make sure it is in a secure place, such as inside a mall or an ATM that has glass around. Do not draw money at night when you are drunk or alone. If possible, only draw money when the banks are still open and not from a lone machine on a deserted street corner.

Be aware there is a fee for every withdrawal transaction. It depends on the bank you draw from, and the country, but it is around $4 to $6 per transaction from the local bank. In addition, your own home bank may also add a fee, normally around $3 or so. Thus, a single withdrawal transaction can easily be $10 in total.

Most machines can only dispense up to a maximum of $400 to $500. All countries' ATM's dispense local money, except Cambodia that dispenses US$.

If you are not sure about your pin number, it's better to go to the ATM machines in one of the banks when the bank is open. This way, if the card is swallowed, you can immediately alert security. Card thief is a problem, and you can easily find your account emptied.

Additional things to watch for are card-scanning strips and machines not dispensing your money, as well as fake, torn or old money (especially in Cambodia). Fake US$ are an issue in Cambodia; as well as older $100 notes are not accepted. This is also true of damaged notes. Even a slight tear in a note will have it shunned away. These torn, old, and sometimes fake notes do make it into the ATM's. Inspect your money as soon as you withdraw it, and if suspect, take your withdrawal slip and immediately go to the bank. In Sihanoukville in Cambodia, venders will often try to flog you old and torn US notes, some will take them back, but this money will be useless to you in other towns in Cambodia – always ask for undamaged notes.

Take note that some backpackers run cons by drawing money, and then swap it for fake notes. They then going to the bank and claim that the ATM dispensed it. Thus, you are not always guaranteed of having your money exchanged, if it really happens to you as the banks are wising up to the con. Some backpackers also run a con and inform the bank that the ATM did not dispense the money, which could be true – but is mostly a lie. Thanks to these conning backpackers, you may be refused help if it actually happens to you.

Be aware of card scanning strips. Before you insert your card, check if the machine has been tampered with. There will normally be an additional strip where you insert your card into the ATM. This reads the numbers on your card. A small camera is normally hidden at the top of the ATM and records you entering your pin number. This is a real problem in Asia, especially in Cambodia. With this information, they can draw money from your account, as if they had your card. The next thing you know, your account has been emptied and there is not much you can do about it. I personally spoke to a number of backpackers whom this happened to. Draw from an ATM inside a bank or shopping mall.

Receiving Funds

If you run dry, and need to receive funds on the go, the best option would be for someone to deposit money directly into your debit or credit card at your local bank back home. If this is impossible, the next-best option is to use a PayPal account and have the money transferred to your bank account. I suggest you set up a PayPal account before you leave home and link it to the card you will be using on your travels, especially if you intend to long term backpack. If this is impossible (in some countries, PayPal accounts do not pay out), then there are money transfer services such as MoneyGram, Union Pay, and Western Union, but they tend to be expensive, and they do not have branches in all the cities. You can use the following links to see where the nearest branch is.

https://secure.moneygram.com/locations
http://www.unionpayintl.com/en/
For union pay use the java scrip popup box to search for a merchant.
http://locations.westernunion.com/

Carry Emergency Cash

Depending on the length of your trip, you may have with you all your funds in cash, or draw money as you go. However, always have at least US$100 in cash tucked away somewhere as emergency money – I suggest 5 x $1 notes, 5 x $5 notes, 3 x $10 notes and 2 x $20 notes.

For trips into the countryside or up into the mountains, I suggest to carry at least $400 in cash with you, or as much as your hotel fees and food. For Cambodia US$ is good, but for the others, you need local currency in the countryside. Do split the money up, hide them in different places, and tell no one of the cash you have with you.

Money Exchange

Do not exchange money at the airport and definitely not at the border unless you have to. Do not believe the border posts, telling you whatever money you have is not used in the country. Anything but local currency and US$ may not be used in the country. However, the border posts and most airports give very poor exchange rates. Actually, borders are mostly rip-offs: at times giving only 50% or less of the exchange rate.

If you have to exchange, only exchange the minimum of what is needed to pay for your visa and bus ticket, if you need to buy one. You can exchange the rest later at an exchange service or normally at hotels and some restaurants at a far better rate. In Cambodia, US$ is the preferred currency so do not exchange US$ to Riel when entering Cambodia.

You do not need loads of $1 bills for Cambodia. Tuk tuk rides are no longer $1, and you can easily pay with a $20 note for most things, or even a 50 or $100 note. If they do not have change, sit tight, they will quickly go out to a neighbor and get change. Simply, do not try to buy a bunch of bananas or a soda with a $100 note – it is rude.

Fake Money

As in many places in the world, fake money does the rounds. However, it is a bit of a problem in Asia. So carefully check your money – $10 and 20 notes are the most common fakes. These are mostly handed out at night and by street vendors. Old and torn $50 and $100 notes are not accepted by anyone as payment.

Traveler's Checks

For the most part, forget about traveler's checks. Only large banks accept traveler's checks, and it costs you money to exchange them. If you have any, go to the larger banks in town and get them exchanged, before you head out to the countryside or smaller towns. Understand there is often a fee charged per check cashed, and not per transaction. Thus, it is better to take larger checks to save on charge fees if you do take any.

Checks

Forget about paying by check, not only is it expensive and old school, but you will be hard-pressed to find any bank that will accept a check, let alone a hotel or shop. Get with the times and get plastic.

Hide and Seek

Never have all your cash in your wallet, and never tell other backpackers how much money you have on you, or in your bank account. There are backpackers who make a living out of stealing, and then there are the opportunists. Know that there are only so many places to hide your money and cards, and with enough time, it will be found if you leave it unattended. From my experience, a few good spots to hide a $100 note or two, that will fool most opportunists, are in used lip ice tubes, pinned behind the inside flap of baseball hats, around the battery of a flashlight or device if there is space, and inside inner linings of backpacks if they can be zipped open (normally backpacks with inner backpack support).

Chapter 11: Dressing Up

The first thing you have to understand about Asia, is that you will be judged and labeled according to the clothes you wear. Asians put a lot of emphasis on their appearance, so much so that people sometimes get work positions entirely on how they dress. If you look the part, there is no reason why you would not be the person you dress up as.

Thus, if you do not want to be treated like a criminal and spot-checked in Asia, especially in Thailand, do not dress like a hippy or a punkster. If you dress like one, expect to be treated like one. You will most likely be searched at random for drugs, and may be asked for a urine sample on the spot, especially in Bangkok. Cambodia is a bit more relaxed, but still customs and police do treat you differently. You are also more likely to be ripped off, and less likely to get good service. Another thing is if you do get in trouble; do not expect the law or others to help you if you look like a scruffy backpacker. Asia has come to look down on backpackers who are just barflies: leaching off everyone, drinking the day away, and caring for no one. Asian thinking is that, if you dress like a barfly, you must be one.

You do not need to bring a whole wardrobe of fancy clothes. Simple clothes such as T-shirts are cheap in Asia ($2 to $5). There are also a number of boutiques in most large towns and many sell traditional clothing that are very nice and cheap. Do note however, that if you are a bit larger than the average Asian, then you may find it difficult getting your size.

Inspect the clothes thoroughly, as many are knockoffs, or damaged stuff thrown out of the factory. Most of the problems you will find are stitching coming loose. Furthermore, know that sizes differ a lot between brands. Even wearing a size 32-inch waist, you may find it hard to fit in pants labeled 42. Take your underwear or pants, and lay the hip seam on the inside of your arm from the fold by your elbow towards your pulse. In the shops, lay out underwear or pants the same way to see if they are the size you are looking for.

What to Wear

Due to it being very hot most months, cool long-sleeve shirts are recommended, including a good sun hat. Wear long sleeves to avoid sunburn. I suggest long pants, or a lot of sun block. I have seen many badly burned legs and faces from a day in the sun. Short sleeves work if you go by tuk tuk, but if you are on the back of a motorcycle for most of the day, wear a long-sleeve shirt, and possibly fingerless summer gloves. Many Chines like to wear thin white material gloves.

I suggest sneakers or closed sandals if you are going to visit any temples in Cambodia. Slops (flip-flops) and high heels are just asking for slipping and falling down in the ruins. In Thailand's temples or pagodas in all countries, you will be asked to remove your shoes before entering. I recommend you wear socks with closed shoes, as your feet will sweat and cause blisters and scuffs from being wet all the time.

Be aware in the wintertime (December – February), the mountain regions, and northern part of Vietnam, gets very cold (5 °C or 41 °F). Remember to take warm clothing if going in the winter to Sapa or any mountain regions.

Underwear

If you intend to stay longer, bring extra underwear. There are few options if you are larger built or well endowed, and the options available are not that great either.

Laundry

Laundry is not a problem, especially in the larger cities. Laundromats can be found everywhere, and most hotels and hostels will be able to wash your clothes for you, even in rural villages. Laundry services, in the regions, runs around $1/kg, and takes a full day. Thus, you will normally get your clothes the next day, unless you pay for express service, which is normally $2/kg of clothes.

Note: do not hand in clothes that are delicate and require special washing instruction or dry-cleaning. Clothes are bundled together in industrial washing and drying machines. Clothes are normally marked with tags. However, it does happen from time to time that a sock or shirt goes missing, or that you get someone else's clothes. Do check your clothes immediately when you get them or back at the hotel, and go back promptly if an item is missing. If you use the same place a few times in a row, you can normally get a discount, as well as special treatment by having your clothes washed faster. Again, do not hand in delicate or special items; whites often come back a different color – rather hand wash them in your room.

If you want to save money, take a piece of thin rope and tie it inside your room as a clothesline. Good places are between windows, or a window to a door or bed. Hand wash your clothes and then hang them on the rope overnight. In summer, even thick denim should be dry after a few hours. You should always check, however, if you are allowed to wash and dry your clothes in your room. Most dorms do not, as they normally have shared laundry facilities you can use. In hotels, or if you have your own room in a dorm, you can normally get away with it, if you wash and dry during the night.

Chapter 12: Travel Insurance

It is a good idea to get travel insurance for your adventure. Although there are many on the market, here are a few suggestions.

Apart from medical emergencies and medical evacuations, you can also insure your laptop, cellphone, camera, and other important items. The more expensive packages normally include coverage for missed flights, for a small additional fee.

World Nomads
Website: *www.worldnomads.com*

AG Cambodia
Website: *www.agcambodia.com*

Aetna International
Website: *www.aetnainternational.com*

April International
Website: *http://en.april-international.com/global*

Insure My Trip
Website: *http://www.insuremytrip.com/*

Chapter 13: Language Problems

Getting past language and cultural barriers is part of traveling, and makes backpacking exciting. If not being able to speak the local language is a concern for you, do not fear. I traveled all over SE Asia and can only speak a few words of Khmer, the official language of Cambodia. I have to admit, that language is not my strong point, yet, it did not stop me from traveling.

In large cities, most hotels will have someone who can speak English. In Cambodia, basic English is spoken by a large percentage of the population, especially by younger Cambodians. You may find that in smaller towns or shops in Cambodia, elders will often call a child to translate. For Laos, Thailand, and especially Vietnam, you may find English is not that common in far-out places. However, even this is not a problem.

There are a number of offline translation applications, and *https://translate.google.com/* is commonly available, even in rural places as the mobile Internet infrastructure is amazing. Look on Apple and Google Play for the country's language you are going to visit.

Cambodia:
https://itunes.apple.com/us/app/lets-speak-khmer/id670835884?mt=8

Vietnam:
https://itunes.apple.com/us/app/learn-vietnamese-phrasebook/id615964822?mt=8

Thailand:
https://itunes.apple.com/us/app/taiwanease/id515864552?mt=8

Laos:
https://itunes.apple.com/us/app/offline-lao-to-english-language/id998853724?mt=8 or
https://itunes.apple.com/us/app/english-lao-dictionary/id906869905?mt=8

It is fun to order food by pointing at "beef", "rice", and "vegetable" on the translation app, and then wait and see what they bring. After some experience, you will quickly start to know the names of the local dishes you like. Most menus have pictures to help you.

Remember you are in a foreign country with different schooling compared to developed countries. Although locals may speak English, do not expect them to understand complex explanations and technical terms, or your laws and expectations from your country. They will rarely admit that they do not understand you. Come to Asia with the expectation that things will not go as planned, and just roll with it.

Chapter 14: Accommodations

Accommodations can be an adventure when backpacking in Asia. You can find very cheap to very expensive rooms. My view is paying more than $25 per room when backpacking is wasting money. The following are some suggestions and tips when booking accommodations:

Prices

For $1 a day, you can get a backpacker bunk at a few places, mostly in Siem Reap, Cambodia or Cowboy Town in Thailand. As the name says, it is basically just a bunk bed, with a shared shower and toilet. You may be lucky enough to have curtains for privacy, or just a mosquito net, leaving you no privacy. These are, however, getting rare, as more places are starting to cater to richer tourists. The dorm will often be outside or made from wood. Bed bugs and hygiene are often problems here, as washed bedding is a joke. Often beds are stacked on top of each other, with no place to store your items safely. The idea is to cram as many beds as possible into a room.

For $2 to $3 a night, you can get a bed in a dorm, with a shared bathroom. The rooms are normally brick construction, and reasonably clean. Bedding is better than the bunk beds, but not much. Normally, dorms will have from 6 to 12 beds in a room, with one fan…if any at all.

For $5 a night, you can rent a room with possibly a ceiling fan, and if lucky, your own bathroom. In more expensive towns, such as Bangkok and Vientiane, $5 a night can get you a room in a clean dorm with air conditioning – and if really lucky – an egg and toast breakfast. If you take a room with a double bed, then it can be a cheap option if sharing with a partner. However, realize that for this price, the room is often not clean and bed bugs are sometimes a problem. $5 per persona a night, in a dorm, is normally clean enough to not have a problem with bed bugs.

For $10 to $15 a night, you can get a room with a double bed and air-conditioning, as well as your own bathroom with hot water. The hotel will normally have free Wi-Fi as well. In guesthouses, this may include breakfast, but in hotels you may need to spend around $20 to $25 a room to have breakfast included.

For $20 to $30, you should easily be able to get a room in a clean and more upmarket hotel, which includes breakfast. You should have your own bathroom with hot water, Wi-Fi, and air-conditioning. If not, then you are being ripped off – look elsewhere.

Anything above $30 a night per room is luxury, although there are hotels that ask above $400 per room. If you are backpacking, paying more than $30 a night for a room is throwing good travel money away.

Do note that outside of larger cities, your options become more limited. However, the prices seem to come down, and standards improve. For accommodations out in the bush, you may find either one of two options, very expensive tourist hotels, or cheap backpacker places. Check what is available before you go.

For long-term backpacking, you may want to look at renting a room from locals or making a deal with a hostel or hotel. I rented a room for initially $80 a month, which was later reduced to $60 a month, from a local Cambodian family. This is a rare find, but for $80 to $100 you should easily find a room in Cambodia, and for $150 a month you should be able to find an air-conditioned room in Cambodia. These prices are around the same in Thailand. Vietnam and Laos (Vientiane) are a bit more expensive, but the quality is better. Bet on approximately $200 to $250 a month (minimum) for a room – most come with furnishings.

Look around for cheap hotels, as hostels are often the same or more expensive than a small hotel. Due to hostels being so popular, many have upped their prices, especially if they have a good location, like being on the beach or near the river. I have had air-conditioned rooms, with hot water, in small hotels two roads away from popular backpacker hostel. I found them to be less money than the hostels, which had no fans, inside bathrooms, or hot water.

What Is That Smell?

Often, old hotels have a problem with plumbing. This is common in Cambodia. It seems the toilet is linked to the shower drain, and at times the toilet smell comes out of the shower drain, especially in the wet months. Check the shower before taking the room, and look for mold or dampness. If something does not smell right when you are shown the room, do not trust that the smell will go away if you open a window – ask for another room.

Yes, We Have Wi-Fi

Many smaller places will tell you that they have Wi-Fi. First, check that it works before taking the room. Also confirm that you get a signal in the room, if they say there is Wi-Fi in the room. On a few occasions I've found they only have one Wi-Fi router, and it reached just a few rooms on the first floor. At times, I had to sit on stairs to Skype at night. You should also double-check what the Wi-Fi connection's name is. I have found them to use the connection from the hotel next door, and not even have their own service. If the Internet goes down, there is not much you can do if you are pirating it from next door.

Booking Online

Walking into a hotel or guesthouse and making a booking on the spot is usually more expensive than making a booking online. So too, is having a travel agent make a booking for you. If possible, try to book online beforehand. However, do note that not all places are listed on Internet sites, so you may have to do some legwork to find their Internet page. Making a booking online or by e-mail is perfectly safe…most of the time. ☺

Personally, I use a number of applications on my iPhone: *http://www.expedia.com/*, *http://www.bookings.com/* and *http://www.hostelhero.com/* (great for backpackers). You can also try *http://www.hotels.com*.

Don't expect an immediate response, or any at all, from backpacker places and smaller hotels if you E-mail them. It's a better idea to phone. Furthermore, check that they have everything you need and that there are English-speaking staff members. However, take note that at times, many of the listed amenities may not work, or no longer be available, when you get there; such as a $10 a night room that is listed with a bath. Baths are a bit rare in Asia, especially in Cambodia and often only found in older or more upmarket and expensive hotels.

Checking In

When you check into your hotel, bring your confirmation number or E-mail with you, as it will make things a lot easier. Many places have an electronic system, but some still use a paper system. *Always check the room, before you agree to take it.* You may be shocked what the room looks like compared to the online ads. Seeing the room before accepting is normal, and helps to avoid later arguments. If you are refused to see the room first, before agreeing to take it, walk away – honestly – actually run.

If you did not book online, book and pay for only one night, and reserve the right to extend your stay. If things are not as you expected (no warm water, air-conditioner not working, place infected with bed bugs), you will likely not get a refund should you want to go to another hotel. You may also not be allowed to change rooms unless you upgrade the room.

In the room, inspect everything. Especially lights, fans, and air conditioners. Furthermore, check that the warm-water unit (if fitted) in the bathroom actually works. In summer, they have a tendency to turn it off to save money, and you are told you don't need it (even if you pay for it). If you find anything not working, immediately complain and either have it fixed (blown light bulb) or have them move you to another room. You'll find once you are in and paid, it is sometimes a bit harder to get another room or have repairs made. Also check for toilet paper, and confirm the toilet flushes. In most of the upper guesthouses and hotels, you will find few problems; however, I did have an air conditioner not working in a hotel and hot water not working in two hotels, in addition to blown fluorescent lights in a number of others.

Scams

An important thing to note is some places may not, at the end of your stay, honor your online booking price, or even the walk in price you agreed to. Stand your ground and always keep your online booking confirmation. Note, that in some case, they may try to ask the full amount, even if you already paid a deposit. You may also be given a bad conversion rate if they convert the online booking fee (normally given in US$), to local currency, and refuse to take anything but local currency. This is rare, but does happen and has happened to me a few times. Just politely stand your ground, but be flexible (especially for conversion rates).

Many hotels, especially in Vietnam, will ask to keep your passport. The only way to get around this is to pay upfront for the room. At larger hotels and hostels, your passport is normally safe. If you do not want to leave your passport, book and pay for only one night, check the room out, and if you are happy, then book and pay for the rest of your stay.

Bringing Someone Home

If you bring a local home, you, in many cases, need to report this to the front desk (fellow tourists are normally fine). The reason is that most locals, especially in Cambodia and Thailand (women normally), that are willing to go to your place for the night are sex workers. Regardless of what they say, they will most likely expect compensation in the morning. This does not mean you cannot pick up a local girl who is not a sex worker, juts note that it is rare for them to follow you home on the first date. In addition, if you met her on the street corner or a bar, she most likely is a sex worker or wants to marry you for your money. Ladies, do be careful of local men on expensive motorcycles (anything other than an older scooter), especially if they speak English. They are either sex workers or money suckers (someone has to pay for that motorcycle).

Voltage

The electricity supply in Asia is around 220v at 'around' 50 Hz (around, because it is not that stable). Power cuts do happen in larger cities, especially Cambodia.

All plugs take two-prong flat blade plugs, the same as in USA. However, they can also accept round pin plugs, but not UK angled flat blades. Adapters are available in larger shops in major cities. Yet, AC 220 to 110v step down converters are not so easy to find, so get an international charger or bring your own voltage converter along.

Long Stay

If you plan to stay for a few months, use Facebook to search for groups associated with the town where you intend to stay. Ask if there are rooms to rent, in a house with fellow travelers or expats for the time you will be in town. You can often find a room for a good price, even if it is only for two weeks or a month. You may also find your own flat for cheap, with a two to three months rental contract.

Wait, I am Booking a Room

I have, at times; arrived at a hotel I liked, and then used their Internet to quickly search on Bookings.com for their ad. With online booking, they have to compete against other ads, and pay a commission, so they lose a lot. I then used the ad and asked the reservation desk if I can get the same rate as they advertise online. No one has refused me yet, and if they do, I just quickly book online. Often, you can save $3 to $10 a night, depending on the price of the room. The hotel still gets more than if you booked online, for they do not have to pay a commission to the booking site.

Chapter 15: Bed Bugs

Major note, especially for cheap backpacker places, always check for BED BUGS. My first two weeks in Cambodia were crap. I booked a room for $5 a night at a backpacker place and found it to contain bed bugs the first evening. It was infested, and the place would not refund me (I had paid upfront for two weeks). I then upgraded to their most expensive unit at $12 a night, and found it to contain bed bugs as well. I had to put up with it, as they refused to refund me again.

Bed bugs are very difficult to get rid of, and can ride along in your luggage, you, or your bags. I had to throw away a lot of stuff that were infested with bed bugs and possible eggs.

The more hostels, and even hotels you use, the bigger the chance of you encountering bed bugs, especially if you use hostels. A sure sign there are bed bugs are bite marks on other backpackers. Unlike mosquitoes that bite you all over, bed bugs leave bite marks in a line, usually three or more. This is due to them feeding on you a bit, moving a short distance away, and then feeding again.

It is possible for one room to be infected, and the next one not. However, bed bugs do travel a large distance if there is no one to feed on in the room they are in.

Do not put your bags on the ground or bed. I stored mine in black trash bags in the shower. Look for small bloodstains on blankets and pillows, little critters under the mattress, as well as looking for and smelling for their fecal matter – with a bad infestation, it may smell sweet or rotting.

As always, if you actually see bed bugs, then the room is infested. Go to another hotel. As mentioned before, do not accept the room before inspecting it, and book for only one or two nights. You will be hard-pressed to get a refund if you pay upfront and do not want the room.

Anton Swanepoel

If you found bed bugs, inspect every one of your items carefully. Know that they climb into laptops and other electronic devices that have openings. You can have all your clothes washed and dried at a Laundromat, as soap and heat kills them, and then seal all your clean clothes in plastic bags. Get medical alcohol (rubbing alcohol) from a chemist (drug store) and a plastic spray bottle. Spray all your bags with medical alcohol, wetting the seams and inside pockets. The alcohol removes the thin layer of wax from their bodies when it comes in contact with them, and they dry out and die. I have sprayed my bed sheets and myself with medical alcohol at night, yielding good results of not being bitten. Most insecticides, sprayed around the bed, bedposts and bedding, seem not to deter them from biting. I have also used organic bed bug repellant, and it worked like water – as in did nothing. I sprayed the stuff all over the bed, and even in one room, directly on bed bugs crawling towards me, and they simply ignored it.

On one occasion, I ran brown cellotape around the edges of the bedding to create a smooth surface, hoping to make them fall off as they climbed up. I then made a ridge, with the tape turned around, to make a sticky bump they had to climb over if they made it over the smooth sides. That worked, and in two weeks I did not get one bite. With wooden ceilings, you may need to run strips larger than the bed against the ceiling, to make the bed bugs fall off before they get over your bed, as they will drop down from the ceiling onto you.

You can also use double-sided tape on the bed legs, while making sure no bedding touches the floor. In addition, put you bed's legs in trays of water or cooking oil. This is after you checked that the bed is clean of bed bugs, and the bed is not against the wall. Bed bugs are attracted to heat and co2 you breathe out.

Note that the bite marks can grow quite big, and if you scratch the bite marks, they can become infected. Some people have little or no reaction to the bites, and reactions may occur days after being bitten.

As well, there are small, pesky, harmless bugs in Cambodia that looks very much like bed bugs, but they have wings. Bed bugs do not have wings and they cannot jump. Bed bugs range from the size of a pinhead to about the size of an apple seed. Adults are brown if they have not fed, and turn reddish brown after feeding. Nymphs and non-adults are whitish before feeding and often blend easily with the mattress.

It is not because hostels are dirty (some may be) that you find bed bugs. It is the sheer volume of customers who give them a greater chance of being infected. A single bedbug can travel on a suitcase or backpack, and put up house in a new location. Bed bugs have even been found in posh hotels in Manhattan, New York. Bed bugs are not unique to backpacking and hostel travel; they are part of travel, like losing passports and missing flights. Just prepare and look out for them, and you will have happy, bite-free travels. At the very least, know that they carry no disease, and if you treat the bites, they will normally go away with no ill effect to you. Some travellers care nothing for being bitten and happily sleep in bed bug-infested places because it is cheap, while claiming the bites are okay or just mosquito bites.

Chapter 16: Transportation

Transportation can be a real experience in SE Asia, especially if you travel between towns. The main transport in Asia is by motorcycle (scooters). Following that, tuk tuk's are next on the list, followed by buses. You can get a car or minibus taxi in some places. However, they are expensive, unless you have a few people paying together. If you are inexperienced at riding on a motorcycle, do not try to climb on with all your backpacks, rather take a tuk tuk. Ask around your tour bus and try to team up and share a tuk tuk to the same or close by hostel or hotel from your bus stop.

Prices

Tuk tuk prices vary widely from tuk tuk to tuk tuk, and also from town to town. However, in most respects, they are cheap. Note that in Shihanoukville, Cambodia there is a price fixing mafia, and it is, in most respects, cheaper to rent a motorcycle than to rent a tuk tuk. In Bangkok, you will run into many tuk tuk scams – see the chapter on popular scams for more information. For short rides, expect to pay around $1 to $2 for a motorcycle taxi, and around $3 to $5 for a tuk tuk. For longer rides, you can easily pay $15 for a tuk tuk. However, sharing a tuk tuk is the cheapest way to travel in town, and by bus for long travels.

Negotiate beforehand on the total price, including all stops, knowing that if you add additional stops, the price may go up drastically. Drivers, who speak English and wait outside malls, guesthouses, and bus stops, are normally far pricier than if you walk a distance away and get a passing taxi.

City-to-City Travel

In Cambodia, your best option between cities is bus travel. In the wet season, if you feel adventurous, you can go by boat. In Thailand and Vietnam, a train ride is a good option. Do, however, take a sleeper bunk bed, as the wooden bench seats are crap on trains. Try to avoid overnight buses, unless you are pressed for time and want an adventure. In Laos, except for from Vientiane to Bangkok, bus travel is your best option. If you are a few backpackers together, you can hire a private car or minivan for a reasonable price.

Booking a ticket on a bus or train is very easy. Most hostels and hotels will be able to book a ticket for you. Do know that there can be a marked difference between a $6 and an $8 bus ride. You will also find many small roadside shops selling bus tickets, especially in Cambodia. For the most part, they sell the same tickets that you get from hostels, but some are frauds. Be wary of buying a bus ticket from a person in a rundown shack. The train ride between Hanoi and Saigon is worth it. For trains in Vietnam, go to the station yourself, or use a good travel agent. Some of the more reliable companies to use are:

http://www.baolau.vn/
http://www.vietnamimpressive.com/
http://www.vietnamtrain.com/
http://www.trainticketdeliver.com/
http://sinhcafe.com/index.htm

The official Vietnamese Railways website is www.vr.com.vn and currently does not accept online bookings. Any website claiming to be the official site, and doing online bookings, is a scam. There are many scam, train-booking websites. Be careful in using a booking service, as often you will pay for a soft sleeper bunk, only to find out when you get your ticket that you have been booked a hard bench. Your train ride will be the equivalent of sleeping two days on a park bench.

Almost all bus services offer pickups at your hotel. Some include it in the price; some may add $1 or so. If you prefer to meet the bus at the bus station, then it will probably cost you $5 in tuk tuk fees. I suggest you opt for being picked up. Always take the number for the bus company, so you can call if you are not picked up at the allotted time. Do not wait for the pick up to be 10 or 15 minutes late before you call. I once waited 10 minutes before I called, as I was used to the driver being late, and was told that they forgot about me (rare to happen). The bus had already left and all they could do was book me on the next available bus, which was the next day.

Remember to keep your bus ticket, as you may be asked on the next stop to produce it, and not be allowed back on the bus if you don't have it. You may also need to show the ticket to get your luggage. Cambodia seems a lot more relaxed and I have done a few bus rides with only a hand written note of "one P, paid". However, Vietnam and Thailand are a lot stricter, with some Vietnam places having multiple checkpoints for each station.

Sitting For Ladies

If you are using a motorcycle taxi, and have never ridden as pillion (passenger) be very careful of the exhaust. It is on the right-hand side, at the back of the motorcycle, and can leave nasty burns that can get infected. Women normally sit sidesaddle, but this is a skill you need to learn as you can easily fall off. Asians will understand if you cannot sit sidesaddle, or do not want to, so go ahead and straddle the seat. You may want to leave the miniskirt and tight pants at home – not that us blokes don't love looking at your sexy legs, but you may find it difficult to climb off gracefully. You run the risk of face-planting yourself onto the roadway, which may prove to be quite unpleasant.

Renting a Motorcycle

If you want to ride yourself, then you can easily rent a motorcycle in most cities in Cambodia (Siem Reap is more expensive). In Vietnam, you can easily buy a second-hand motorcycle or rent one. Laos is a bit harder to rent a motorcycle outside Vientiane and other large towns, and they are expensive. In Thailand, outside of Bangkok, you can rent motorcycles, but in Bangkok, renting a motorcycle is a problem.

Prices for motorcycles depend on the type of motorcycle, and where you are. However, on average, in Cambodia and Vietnam, you can expect to pay around $5 a day for a scooter. Vientiane was around $8 a day. For dirt bikes, you can easily pay $30 and up per day.

Renting a Bicycle

Renting a bicycle is one of the cheapest options for getting around. Almost all guesthouses and backpacker places rent out bicycles. Some even include rental with your room rate. Rentals go from around $1 a day to $5 – anything more than $2 a day is expensive.

Take time to check that the tires are fully inflated and not smooth. Get one with a carry basket in front, and a fitted light, if you want to ride at night. Furthermore, get a lock so that you can lock it up in town.

Traffic

Traffic is organized chaos in SE Asia. So if you are in a tuk tuk, sit back and enjoy the view. If you are on the back of a motorcycle, hold on. And if you are cycling or riding yourself, go slow, watch out all around you, and go with the flow. Expect people to fly past you from all sides and cut in front of you. Use your indicators, but do not rely on them, or the intention of flashing indicators from other road users. Rather use your arms to signal where you want to go. Often it is the passenger, at the back, who does the signaling. Expect anything, with larger wheels than you, to not care about you and push their right-of-way.

Roads between cities can become dangerous, especially between Siem Reap and Phnom Penh, Cambodia. Do not attempt city-to-city trips unless you have good riding experience or someone to guide you. Do expect roads to deteriorate quickly during the rainy season, as potholes form. Watch out for sand patches all over.

Maps

Street names and numbers have changed so many times that different generations of maps will have different names. Names are also translated differently from local languages to English.

It is best to use an electronic map with a GPS enabled phone. The best I found is ForeverMap. Try *https://itunes.apple.com/us/app/forevermap-2-worldwide-offline/id424183595?mt=8*

Do not expect the locals to be able to read maps (especially in English) or to know the names of places by heart. If you can show them a picture of the place, it will be easier.

Accidents

Accidents, like all over the world, do happen, and if it does, expect a crowd to gather quickly. Do not get angry if you are involved. Know that you will probably be blamed, and expected to compensate the other driver (victim). Police may actually try to push this amount higher so that they can get a nice commission as well.

If you are injured seriously, be aware that calling an ambulance is expensive, so if you can get to a hospital by tuk tuk, use it. If a local calls for an ambulance, they normally get a commission of up to $50 for calling, and it will be included in your bill. If you are out cold, you may be relieved of the burden of your possessions.

Know that, even if you are right, thinking you are going to fight it out in court will get you nowhere…but maybe jail. Just smile, be polite, and negotiate the amount down. (An older secondhand scooter sells for around $300 to $600, newer up to $2200, just to give you an idea of bargaining prices.

Legally, you need a local driving license, so you are at fault even if it was not your fault. Few rental places bother to see a driving license if you rent a scooter, that is until you are involved in an accident, and then it is fully your fault. Read the rental contract carefully, as you may be expected to pay $500 to $2000 if you are involved in an accident, no matter how slight the damage on the scooter is.

Rental places often keep your passport, so there is no real way out. Never ever, try to run from a rental place after being involved in an accident. Thinking you will go to the consulate and claim you lost your passport, and then get a temporary one and skip town is stupid. That is fraud, and the police will already have your old passport and flag you as a criminal at all border crossings and airports.

When Drunk

If you are going out to party, arrange with your hotel for a taxi to come pick you up. Moreover, do not use motorcycle taxies when drunk. Know that tuk tuk taxies are scarcer late at night. Get the number of a tuk tuk driver you have used and arrange for him to come and pick you up. Falling off a motorcycle taxi when drunk or getting into an accident is one of the major causes of tourists getting hurt in SE Asia.

General Travel Times and Prices

Travel times vary widely; depending on the service you take, as well as the road conditions and weather. Prices are also a thing that fluctuates widely. However, here are a few prices that I paid to give you some idea.

Bangkok to Siem Reap: $24 on a luxury bus and minivan, about eight hours travel time. You can get buses as low as $16.

Siem Reap to Phnom Penh: From $6 to $24, and about an eight hour trip. $12 rides seem to be the best for price and luxury.

Phnom Penh to Kampot or Sihanouville: Around $8 and about four to five hours. Buses to Kampot often stop at Kep first. I got a sleeper bus back from Sihanoukville to Siem Reap for $12, but will not do it again. ☺

Siem Reap to Saigon: $24 for a good bus and around a 12-hour ride.

Siem Reap to Poipet border: $6 and around three hours in a minivan. Same from Siem Reap to Battambang.

Siem Reap to Vientiane in Laos: 48 hours and about $50. This was a crapshoot and instead I would suggest you to take a bus to Bangkok and then a bus or train to Vientiane. I was dropped just beyond the Laos border at 6pm and told my connecting bus would be there soon. By 8pm I flagged another tour bus down and was told there is no connecting bus until the next morning at 8am. I got a ride to Pakse, overnighted there and fought the bus company to give me a ticket from Pakse to Vientiane.

Saigon to Hanoi: About $50 and 42 hours by train in a sleeper section with four beds. You can get cheaper bunks, but I do not recommend it.

Bangkok to Ayutthaya: The trip is $4 by minivan and around three hours, including stops.

Chapter 17: Internet and Cell Phone Service

Southeast Asia has a surprisingly good cell phone and Internet service, with 3.5G readily available in major cities, and even acceptable speed in smaller villages. The services are improving day-by-day, with faster speed and larger coverage.

Free Internet

Most hotels and guesthouses have free Wi-Fi connection; although most rooms do not have LAN connections. The coverage and Internet speed does depend on the hotel, with more upmarket places providing coverage in the rooms, while others, such as guesthouses and backpacker places, only providing coverage by the bar, lobby, reception, and maybe dining places. Most hotels, and nearly all guesthouses and backpacker places, have at least one shared computer that you can use, but do not bargain on it.

There are a number of Internet shops in larger towns, especially close to backpacker hostels. These shops can, in addition to providing you with a PC to use, normally do color printing, CD copying, and data burning. Although, sometimes you may need to help the staff operate a computer.

In Cambodia, almost all restaurants and larger dining places, will have free Wi-Fi. In Vietnam, Laos, and Thailand, it seems to be only the bigger restaurants that have Wi-Fi, and on the road very few roadside eatery places have any Internet connection at all.

More upmarket buses in Cambodia, at times, have Internet, but I have found it to be unreliable and slow at best. A better option would be to get your own SIM card with mobile Internet.

Cellular Data Connection

Connection to the Internet through an SIM card is by far the easiest and best option when backpacking South-East Asia.

There are a number of cellular providers in each country. You will normally pay around $3 to $5 for the SIM card. If you go to an official shop, you will be asked to show your passport. It may also be cheaper to get a SIM card from another backpacker who is leaving the country.

Ask the provider what the current data packages are, as out of bundle prices are very steep. Normally, you can get a package of approximately 3GB of data for $5 of 3G speed, with unlimited data use after that on a reduced speed. In Cambodia, both Metfone and Cellcard are good, with Cellcard being my preference.

SIM Adapter

Different devices use different size SIM cards. If you want to use one SIM card in multiple devices, which use different-sized cards, get a SIM adapter. This is needed if you have an iPad, as you cannot send a text message from an iPad to recharge your account and will need to put it in a cellphone. (Cellcard in Cambodia have an IPad app that allows you to recharge from the IPad).

Automatic Renewal

Most providers, especially in Cambodia, allow for automatic renewal of your prepaid data packages. For instance, load $20 on your card and then enjoy hassle-free service for four months at $5 a month. Check with the provider you choose in the country you are in, as services and prices, as well as providers, change so fast, giving prices and links here is of no use.

Vietnam Cellular

Vietnam has a number of service providers. Some of the better ones are
http://vinaphone.com.vn/locale.do?language=en
http://www.mobifone.vn/wps/portal/public
http://vietteltelecom.vn/index.php/
You can get a local SIM data card at the airport, or all larger cities.

Utilize an official store to get a SIM card, if you are getting one in the city, as smaller shops may overcharge you by a lot. Ask your hotel or hostel's reception where the nearest official shop is. One of the best shops to go to is www.thegioididong.com. Vinaphone offers what seem to be the best packages, starting from $0.50c for 50mb. The unlimited plan for 50K VND (at current) is the best option. SMS "DK MAX" to 888, see *http://vinaphone.com.vn/services/mobiinternet#cuocphi-tab* for more information. You get 600mb at 3G speed, then unlimited at normal speed. To set up GPRS, SMS "GPRS" to 333: APN (Access Point Name) settings are - APN: m3-world, User: mms, Password: mms. (This may change without notice).

Cambodia Cellular

There are two good providers in Cambodia, namely Cellcard and Metfone.

Cellcard

http://www.cellcard.com.kh
http://www.cellcard.com.kh/cellcard-internet
Cellcard offers a tourism SIM card, and is a good option if you want to call abroad, as it is currently 4.5 cents per minute to selected countries. Good data plans are $5 for 3.5 GB or $10 for 8 GB, both at 3.5G speed.
$5 plan, dial #6767#500#
$10 plan, dial #6767#1000#
To Top Up, dial *123*14-digit code#
Check your balance, dial #124#

APN setting is cellcard, with no password or user name. You can create a hotspot.

Metfone

http://www.metfone.com.kh/en/Home/Default.aspx
http://www.metfone.com.kh/en/Services/Mobile-Internet-3G-Pacakge/Mobile-Internet-Package.12.aspx

Metfone is more expensive than Cellcard but a far better service provider, with $5 giving you 2.5GB, and $10 providing you with 5 GB, however their unlimited package is the best. For $3 a month, you get unlimited data (1.5GB at 3.5G speed, then capped at 256kb/s. Still fast enough for Skype). I use the $5 plan, and when I need extra speed to download or upload large files, I add an extra 3G data to my account at $1 for 600mb.

$3 plan dial *133*4# (Monthly plan unlimited data)
$5 plan, dial *133*50# (Monthly plan unlimited data)
$10 plan dial *133*100# (Monthly plan unlimited data)
0.5c added data of 250mb @ 3G speed, dial *133*3#
$1 added data of 600mb @ 3G speed, dial *133*9#
To Top Up, dial *197*pin number#
Check Balance, dial *097#
Customer Care, dial 1777

Thailand Cellular

Data SIM cards are readily available at the airports, as well as in most towns in 7-11's. Cellular data connection is cheap in Thailand. You need an unlocked phone that can take a SIM card and operate in any of these bands, GSM 850, 900, 1800, and 2100MHz (operator dependent). The three main service providers are:
http://www.ais.co.th/
http://www.happy.co.th/home_en.php
http://www.truemove.com/en

AIS and DTAC give the best coverage outside of larger centers. AIS offers a 1GB Internet package for 123 Baht a week. Truemove offers a 2GB package for 399 Baht. DTAC offers an unlimited Internet (1.5GB at max speed then reduced speed) for seven days for 299 Baht or a 15 day, 4GB plan for 599 Baht. You can order this package at *http://store.dtac.co.th/en/happytouristsim* and pick it up at the airport (Suvarnabhumi Airport, Gate 7).

Chapter 18: Etiquette

Although your stay may be short in SE Asia, do realize that your effect on the people will carry on in their lives, and possibly the lives of their children. Things you may take for granted can have devastating effects on locals. Such as being rude, losing your temper or shouting. Shouting and losing control is the ultimate in losing face, and embarrassment to Asians. Be mindful of your reactions, smile, take a deep breath and try to resolve the situation in a different way.

Clothing
Many tourists walk around in shorts and cut-off shirts. Some men go without shirts, and some women walk around in bikinis (away from the beaches). Cambodian people are very tolerant, Thailand less so, and in Vietnam expect to be stopped. You are not going down to the local Wal-Mart, dress properly. Know that it is disrespectful to enter a Pagoda without a white or blue shirt, not taking your shoes and hat off, and not wearing pants that cover your knees, and shirts that do not cover your shoulders. Some Pagodas will allow you in, but others may stop you at the door if the shirt or pants are too short. Miniskirts are out. At some places, you may be able to rent or buy covers, but at others, like the top of Angkor Wat, you cannot, and will be turned away. Remove your shoes when entering Pagodas or someone's house, even if there is no sign stating so.

Hands
Many tourists greet servers and cashiers by placing their hands by their eyes, mouth, or even worse, brow. Such gestures are embarrassing for the person. A sign of high respect, given by touching chest or mouth are for you, from the server, yours back should be around your stomach or heart. A hand-by-your-brow greeting is reserved for the Buddha or royalty (greet monks this way as you are giving respect to Buddha). As well, give and take things with your right hand.

Touching

Refrain from touching servers, cashiers, or local women you may encounter. Asia is not as open as other cultures, and it is considered harassment. Even if the server does nothing (most probably because they do not want to embarrass you or them by making a scene that will probably get them fired), please do not do it.

Furthermore, respect local woman's space and do not stand too close to them or look straight into their faces. Any of these actions will make the woman feel very uncomfortable. (Younger women who deal with tourists are slowly changing things). Women, never touch a Monk, not even his mother may. Women are normally required to place any item they want to give on a tray, and hold the tray for the monk to take it. Grabbing a monk and wanting to get a picture with him may result in an embarrassing situation.

Saving Face

Asians like to ask you your age and where you are from in the first sentence, when they meet you. They are not being nosy. They are just trying to determine how they should address you, to save you, and them, an embarrassing moment by addressing you incorrectly.

Have respect for the locals. Sometimes they may look at you funny. No, they are not looking at you with disgust or scorn. They are looking at you in wonder and admiration. Think about it, if you flew in, that airplane ticket you paid for could feed them for months. Most of them just dream of climbing on an airplane or bus and going to another country. You are a living example of their dreams. Just because you have more money than them, does not mean they are lower than you. Your actions may result in the next tourist being treated badly. Even though a bus ticket from Siem Reap to Phnom Penh is $6, I have met many locals that have never seen their own capital.

Most people over 50 have seen war and have lost family and friends, be mindful of this. Never lose your cool and shout, scream or curse. Smile and laugh, while you, in a soft tone, discuss your point or try to get the bribe down from the policeman. Asians also do not like to say 'NO', or 'I Don't Know'. They would rather softly say 'yes', or give you incorrect information. This is not lying; it is saving face. Realize that this may be the case, and do not try to push for an answer. It is SE Asia, and you are not going to change a tradition in a day.

I Am Loaded

Do not brag to locals of how much money you have or are making back home. And do not wave loads of cash in their face. They may be poor, but it is no reason to disrespect them. They may just relieve you of the burden of your cash.

I Am Cheap

In Cambodia, and for the most part Thailand, you can negotiate things a bit. In Laos and Vietnam, I found them reluctant to negotiate prices. Although it is suggested to negotiate most of the time, do not do this excessively. I have seen backpackers argue over $1 for a $2 handmade item, and then go and blow $50 on a meal and drinks. You will normally be given a price and if you do not look interested, be given a discount. If a price is given with a sign, then that is normally the lowest the item will sell for. If your tuk tuk driver laughs at your offer and drives away, you insulted him with your offer. Please do not take an item in a shop to the cashier and try to negotiate a lower price. They have no power to give you a discount, and you just look cheap and stupid.

Greeting

It is polite to greet one another in Asia, with the traditional way holding hands together, as in prayer, and the head slightly bowed. Younger people and lesser status people should greet first.

As noted, the higher you place your hands to your brow and the lower you bow, the greater respect you give. Thus, give the greeting to people of equal or higher social standing than you, and monks, not servants, waiters, taxi-drivers, etc.

Always give a proper greeting to Monks, even if it is a kid, as you are actually greeting the divine Buddha in them, and not them. Note that a real monk will normally not return a folded hand greeting, but may give you a blessing.

Some Asians, especially educated or people that deal with many foreigners will take your hand for a handshake. However, still start with a traditional greeting, and do not take a woman's hand to shake it, and please do not try to charm her by kissing her hand. If you do hand something, give it with your right hand, or both if needed, not your left. (You eat with your right and wipe with your left.) If you want to show respect to someone of higher status, support your right elbow with the fingers of your left hand.

Pointing

Pointing, in any sort of way, is extremely rude. Thus, do not point your finger or the soles of your feet directly at a person. Make sure you do not point your chopsticks or fork at another person when you place them down on the table. To ensure you do not point the souls of your feet at someone when you sit on the floor, sit on your legs with your feet tucked back behind. Know that it is rude to cross your legs when you are talking to others.

Pictures

Note that in some places, such as the silver Pagoda in the Palace in Phnom Penh, inside some Pagodas, inside some shops, it is forbidden to take pictures.

Don't take any pictures of logging trucks (honestly, deforesting is a big thing and a few journalist's deaths, being hacked up, made the news not long ago). Do not take pictures of roadblocks, police, or army. In addition, never take a picture of officials or of royalty unless given permission. Note that the numbers 3 and 5 are special to Khmer, so do not take pictures with 3 or 5 people, as it is considered unlucky, and bad fortune may fall upon the person in the middle. Ask if you can take a close-up of locals, and be very wary of taking pictures of children. Child molestation, by foreigners, is a problem in SE Asia, especially in Cambodia.

Chapter 19: Saving Money On Your Trip

Before you start buying anything, you first have to get budgeting under your belt. Running a proper budget is fundamental to long term travel. It is not hard to do; it just takes a different mindset. What you need to realize is what you do today, will affect you later. What you buy, or do not buy, today, will affect your travels for a long time to come. Following are some tips to help you save money.

Know Your Spending

Few people plan a proper budget at home, and less do so on holiday. However, when backpacking on a shoestring budget, running a proper budget plan is paramount to a successful adventure. The best way to do this is by writing down everything you buy. You can use a digital budget application on your phone, or a small notebook. You do not need to write down every item you buy, just the total you spend for the day. At the very least, write down the amounts you draw from ATM machines. You will then have some idea of how much you have left in the bank.

Accommodations

Accommodations are one of your biggest expenses on a trip.
Look on the Internet for hotels and guesthouses giving deals. I have had luxury hotels give 50% or more of a discount, and I stayed in them cheaper than backpacker places. Booking online, as mentioned before, normally is cheaper than walking in and booking a room. If you are not going for a hostel, then try to share a room with a fellow backpacker you like. You can also save if opting for a fan-cooled room instead of air conditioning. Also ask for long-term rental rates, even in hotels. A room going for $5 a night may be yours for $100 per month.

Transport

When booking buses, trains and flights, there are always different classes, and deals to be had. However, going for the cheapest option is not always that smart, nor is going for the top of the line. A $6 bus from Siem Reap to Phnom Penh often breaks down and is not very comfortable, with rarely a working air conditioner. A $24 bus ticket may get you a clean, new bus with working air conditioning, yet you get about the same service on an $8 bus ticket.

Try a motorcycle taxi above a tuk tuk to save money, or share a tuk tuk with other backpackers. Consider walking for short distances and possibly renting a bicycle. For longer backpacking tours, consider buying a $30 bicycle instead of renting one for $1 a day. Just never buy an expensive bicycle (more than $40 second hand) or a new one, as you will often struggle to get it sold unless you take a big loss. As mentioned before, tuk tuks outside hostels and shops are more expensive than getting one further away on the road. If you need a ride for a few days, try to negotiate with a tuk tuk driver for a better rate and share it with other backpackers. Know that you will not get a discount on the first day, as many backpackers say they will take a tuk tuk the next day, and do not. However, on the second day if you show up, the tuk tuk will often give you a better rate.

Food

A tendency for travellers is the desire to eat at all the funky places. This is cool and okay, when you are on a large budget or traveling for a short while. However, it will eat into your budget very fast.

Eating at smaller restaurants and street food vendors will save you loads of cash. Know that some backpacker places are cheap with their rooms, but are normally very expensive with their drinks and meals. This is partly where they make their money. Ones in Kampot are very expensive, as they are far from the town. You can save significantly by buying fruit at local markets, as well as buying food from supermarkets and making your own meals. Note that many hotels and hostel do not want you to make your own food. If they supply a kitchen, then it is okay, else, try cereal with long life milk and bread with cheese spreads, and other items that needs no refrigeration, such as crackers. Do not buy a gas stove and cook in your room without permission. This can get you thrown out of the hostel.

Water

Water is important in SE Asia, and can become expensive if you constantly buy ½ L bottles; instead buy 1.5L bottles of water. Ask around, many shops (especially in Cambodia), allow you to refill your water bottle for cheap, and you can buy 2L bottles for around 50c to $1 in Cambodia, and about the same elsewhere.

Renting

Renting a bicycle or motorcycle from a hostel or hotel is not always the cheapest option. Shop around before you agree and ask for a multi-day rental discount.

Being a Tourist

Oh, that is nice. I have to get that for so and so, and oh, I love this. I just have to have it. The next thing you know, your wallet is empty. Buying useless stuff that is just going to sit on a table, or lie in a drawer, is a good way to go broke.

Another way to blow through your money is to take tourist trips. Going on a tour is expensive. You can save a lot by going to an attraction yourself, rather than taking guides or going on tour packages. Firstly, ask around if a place is worth going to, as some are just tourist traps. Tonle Sap Lake in Cambodia is a huge tourist trap.

Being Social

One of the things that draws so many backpackers to SE Asia, is the cost, especially how cheap alcohol is. Although you want to be social, try some self-control. Clubbing the nights away is a sure way to blow through your budget, as well as your time in Asia. It is also a sure way of getting drugged, robbed, and possibly hooked on drugs. See scams and safety chapters for more information.

Know Where To Shop

Many of the same items are sold all over in each country. If you like something that is locally made, try to buy it away from popular tourist places. Street vendors and small shops, away from backpacker hostels and shopping malls, may help you save a few dollars. There are almost always two markets in any given town – one where tourists are led, and one where locals shop. Learn the local signs for numbers, for if you ask what something costs, while a local price is listed, you will most likely be charged double. If you have or make friends with locals, ask whether they will be willing to buy an item for you that you like. Locals will often be able to negotiate a far better deal for you than if you bought it yourself.

Chapter 20: You and the Law; How to Stay Out of Jail

Be aware that you are subject to local laws, and ignorance is no excuse. Just because you are a tourist, does not put you above local laws. Moreover, forget about your rich uncle that is a judge back home. Unless he has a local lawyer's license and understands local laws, he cannot do much to help you.

It is shocking how many tourist (Australians, Americans, Brits, and French, seem to be at the top of the list from statistics), think that SE Asia is a place where you can do as you please and just pay a bribe. In many regards, SE Asia is very lenient towards tourists when it comes to minor offenses, such as riding a scooter without a local license. However, there are a few things they do not tolerate; such as theft, rape, sex with children, drugs, and slander.

Before I go into more detail, understand that you will often be detained for up to two years, before your case is even heard and you can prove your innocence or pay a fine – so think before acting stupid.

Theft

You may not think about robbing a bank, yet many backpackers do simple, but stupid things, that land them in just as much trouble. Common stupid things are trying to steal small items in shops (many shops in Bangkok have cameras), taking items you think are of no value for souvenirs, such as coasters in a bar, or even public items like blankets on a train. Taking anything, even a coaster in a bar, can result in jail time.

On the train from Vientiane to Bangkok, a backpacker in the seat behind me tried to sneak a blanket out in his backpack when we stopped. Even in the chaos of everyone getting ready to get off, the conductor saw the blanket was missing. Within seconds, police appeared from nowhere and opened his bags. The blanket was found in his main backpack, and he was taken away. His life and travels stopped right there. The penalty for stealing public items is harsher than stealing from a shop.

In 2009, a group of Australian women went clubbing in Phuket. Friends tried to pull a joke and placed a bar mat in one of their friend's handbags, whose birthday it was. She was caught, and although the friends pleaded guilty for placing the mat in her handbag, she was charged and detained. She was facing a possible five-year sentence in a Thai jail. The mother of four was detained for two days in a cramped prison cell, before being released on bail. After 18 days, she pleaded guilty to theft, even though there was video evidence that she was innocent in order to end her ordeal. She was fined and then deported. Later, she would find out she was internationally listed as a criminal when she was denied a visa for the USA. Look up Annice Smoel, for more information.

In Thailand, petty theft is up to three years in jail; this increases to five years if the crime was at night, a break-in, or item used for public benefit; such as the blanket on the train incident mentioned earlier. If it is anything in a holy place, such as a pagoda, items used for public worship, or a Buddha statue, it is up to 10 years in prison.

Claiming You Were Robbed

A favorite among backpackers, especially in Bangkok, is to claim they were robbed. The normal story is that they went out and when they came back to their hotel their items, such as their laptop and camera, were stolen. Often they go to the police to get a police report, and then claim the loss from their insurance. Know that while you are at the police station, they secretly send someone to your room to look for the items. If the items are found in your room or person, you will be charged with fraud and possibly jailed. Accusing a tuk tuk driver or someone else of stealing your stuff may also result in jail time for you, if the items are found in your possession. If you were robbed, go to the police, but do not try to run a con.

Will You Take This For Me?

Drug running is a big business in SE Asia. And the law takes it seriously. Punishment for trying to smuggle cocaine is often life in prison, or in some case death. And yes, foreigners do get executed at times (especially in Malaysia), and there is not much even your government can do about it.

Popular scams include hitting on girls and befriending them, and then asking them outright to take a package or backpack home for them. Too often these packages contain illegal drugs; commonly cocaine. Most of the time, they seek out backpackers who are a bit low on cash, and in a bit of a situation.

Know, that nothing you are currently going through is as bad as life in a Thai prison, or risking your life.

There are other options for getting money to return home. If you have no family or friends, and no one wants to help, you can look at the links given in the chapter for volunteering to teach English. You may even find a job that you love. You can also go to your embassy, and take a loan from them to get you home.

If someone talks about smuggling drugs – walk away. Realize the amount you can carry is not even a blip on the radar of what is actually going through, and you are targeted because you are expendable. If it truly was foolproof and the scanners honestly cannot see the drugs or the customs guy really was paid off, then they would not need you. Furthermore, note that sometimes they pick someone to burn. They give you a few Kg of cocaine to take, and then purposely inform customs that you have drugs. While the custom agents are busy arresting you, the real carrier takes 20 Kg of cocaine past the custom officials. You were the sacrifice to get the other guy through customs. Claiming you knew nothing, is not going to help, you are going to prison for life.

If you were stupid enough to agree to carry the drugs, there still may be a way out. Up until you try to pass customs, you can still go to a toilet and dump it, or turn around and head back. You can drop the suitcase or backpack, if needs be. At times, the customs officers knew the person had drugs, but they waited until the person tried to pass through customs. If you do not try to pass customs, and are caught, you are in possession of drugs. If you tried to pass through customs, you tried to smuggle drugs, a bigger offence.

Watch a few episodes of 'locked up abroad' on YouTube, as well as do a Google search for foreigners locked up due to drug charges. You will soon see it is not worth it. If you are afraid of drug dealers coming after you, I would hide the drugs and then go to an American embassy and tell them your problem before you try to pass through customs. I'm not sure how Asian customs handle it if you inform them you have drugs, but I think American DEA will be more understanding. However, do not keep the drugs with you…whatever you do.

Drugs and Alcohol Use

SE Asia does have a problem with drug and alcohol abuse, but the governments are taking strong steps to change that. They are determined to rid the image of a drug haven. Thus, things are steadily getting more regulated and scruffy places are steadily disappearing, as shops and bars start to cater less to the junky backpacker, and more for the upscale tourist with money.

Two months after I arrived in Siem Reap, Cambodia the police had a major crackdown in town and closed a number of bars after raiding them. The problem was that some bars mixed drugs into the drinks themselves to get the customers hooked on drugs.

One of the big reasons for drug abuse is that it is so readily available; even though it is illegal for you, as a tourist, to use or possess banned substances, such as weed, cocaine, meth, and so on. You will be arrested and jailed if caught with it. Some backpacker places allow guest to use drugs openly (normally smoking weed). However, most will immediately call the police and kick you out if they smell or see drugs. Kampot and Sihanoukville backpacker places seem far more relaxed towards drugs.

If you do take drugs, be very careful of the dose. Drugs are cheaper and sometimes purer in Asia than back home, as the intermediary is cut out. Another thing to note is that heroin is cheaper in Cambodia than cocaine, and you are sometimes given heroin and told it is cocaine. What you may think is a safe amount to use, can easily overdose and kill you. If not, you may just find that you are suddenly addicted to heroin, after just one use. Say good-bye to your life, as very few can quit heroin addiction, even with intense help.

On the flip side is the cheap backyard person that cuts the drugs with anything he can find; from battery acid to drain cleaner. You will have no idea what you are actually taking.

Another thing to watch for, is drug sellers injecting heroin into drunk, passed-out people, just to get them hooked. Being high on drugs, you also run the risk of having your drink spiked, and then being robbed and possibly raped. If you wake up, have more than panties on, and can remember anything, you are lucky. You are even luckier, if you are not in a jail or a hospital when you wake up. Do your pub-crawl at your own risk. Be aware that some of the pot and hash sold may leave you stoned for two days, open to being robbed, or dead (especially drugs sold in Thailand). Never leave your drink unattended or take drinks from people you do not trust. Try to stay sober and do not experiment with drugs, no matter how good you're told you'll feel. It can take just one injection of heroin to be hooked for life.

Following is a short summery of the drug laws for a few countries:

Cambodia: 5 year to life in prison.
Indonesia: 20 years for marijuana offenses and death penalty for narcotics trafficking. Possession of group 1 is four to twelve years.
Laos: Minor drug offenses (soft drugs and under 500 grams heroin) is 10 years in prison. Possessing more than 500 grams of heroin is death by firing squad.
Malaysia: Up to life in prison for possession of less than 15 grams of heroin or less than seven ounces of marijuana. Death if you exceed these amounts or try to cross any border with drugs.
Philippines: Death if caught with at least 0.3 ounce of opium, morphine, heroin, cocaine, marijuana resin, or at least 17 ounces of marijuana. A minimum sentence of 12 years if caught with even 0.17 ounce of illegal drugs.
Singapore: Death penalty for possession of a minimum of half an ounce of heroin, or at least 1 ounce of morphine or cocaine, or at least 17 ounces of marijuana.
Thailand: From life in prison for cocaine and other drugs to the death sentence for heroin.
Vietnam: Death sentence for possession of over 1.3 pounds of heroin. Long jail terms for lesser offences.

Know that you can be imprisoned even if you have drugs on you for personal use. Australian model, Michelle Leslie, was arrested in 2005 and served three months in jail until she pleaded guilty and paid a fine, after she were caught with two ecstasy tablets in Bali, Indonesia. The tablets were found in her handbag on a routine search at an open-air dance party at GWK Park on the Indonesian island of Bali.

Underage Girls

This scam is mostly employed in Thailand, but can happen all over SE Asia. A girl will target a guy, befriend him, and lead him on. She will normally try to get him drunk, and go to his place. They may have sex, or not, but he can be busted for just being naked with her. Then it turns out, she is under aged, and he's hauled off, and thrown in prison. Often, offenders are given a choice of paying a massive fine of a few thousand dollars, or time in prison. The fine is compensation to the girl's family for ruining their honor. If one is lucky, a fine is paid, the passport returned, and the party is kicked out of the country. If not, welcome to 20 or so years in a Thai prison.

A friend of a friend was busted on the beach just kissing a girl. Police showed up and took him away. The next day they apparently had already matched his DNA from supposed sperm in her, and charged him. In the end, after six months in a village police holding station, his dad had to fly over and pay a $15,000 fine to get him out of jail.

Rape Accusations

This can be just as bad, or worse, than the underage girl. A girl, or sometimes group of girls, will lure you and your friends to an apartment. You may have sex with her, protected or not, or just start to undress. If you are lucky, a group of guys will show up, beat the crap out of you and take your money for raping their friend.

If you are really unlucky, you will wake up with the police in your face and the girl claiming you raped her. Even if you used a condom, semen may suddenly be found in her. This one is bad, as they actually will have your semen. You may be lucky to walk away after paying a heavy bribe of thousands of dollars, or you may find yourself in prison for many years to come.

Freedom of Speech

You have the right to say nothing, unless you praise the king and government. Going on Facebook or your blog and saying how corrupt and bad the government is and criticizing the King or government, can get you arrested, jailed, or deported and banned. They can charge you with causing unrest, trying to overthrow the government, or defacing the country and government's image. Even if what you said is true, it can still be viewed as slander. Again, it may not be the fine for slander that gets you. It is the two years you spend in detention while you wait for your case to be heard.

Know that the death penalty is still in effect in Vietnam, and one of the charges you can be executed for is undermining peace and infringing on national security. Although the case for foreigners is normally brought to trail reasonably quickly, most countries, especially Vietnam, have an unlimited pre-trial detention law for people they view as a threat to national security.

Illegal Stuff

Take note that some of the stuff sold in Asia may not be legal in your country. Although rare, one should still check. Things to watch out for are woodcarvings, and leather items from crocodiles or tortoises. Each country's import rules and taxes are different and change, so it is up to you to know what you can import into your country and the tax you need to pay. If in doubt, declare it at the airport customs. Yes, even the leather belt or handbag you bought. It may be of different leather than what you were told, and customs officers will know by looking at it. If it is illegal and you declared it, they will just stop it, and possibly confiscate it. If you did not declare it and it is illegal, you will be charged with smuggling. It is better to declare and pay tax or maybe have it confiscated, than to go to jail. Watch out for leather, feathers, animal products (such as mooty or dried bones), and bat fur or bat products.

Chapter 21: Scams to Watch Out For

In Asia, there are a number of scams that are commonly pulled on unsuspecting tourists and backpackers. Most of the time the scam will leave you short a few dollars, but others can cause lots of problems for you. The bigger scams are under chapter 20. Following are some of the more popular scams that you may encounter.

Visa Scams at Borders

The asking price for visas, at borders, is often not what the official price is. At smaller border posts, you may be taken to a small office where you pay for your visa, only to find out later that it is actually not an official visa, but a scam. Between Thailand and Cambodia, you may be told that the visa can only be paid in Baht, and given a very poor exchange rate from US$ to Baht. Entry and exit stamp fees are also sometimes added, especially between the Laos and Cambodian border. It is best to get a visa beforehand, rather than trying to get one at the border. These scams normally will leave you a few dollars out of pocket, so do not try to make a big scene, just move on. Other times, even though you are right (such as an exit stamp fees of $2), no amount of arguing is going to get your passport stamped without paying the fee. And do you really want to get all red in the face, and start your day angry, over a few dollars?

Stamps at Borders

An uncommon, but problematic scam is for border posts to not actually stamp your passport on entry, or to stamp the wrong date. When you try to leave the country, you will be fined heavily for not having an entry stamp in your passport or for overstaying your visa. Make sure your passport has the correct entry and exit stamp for each border. Furthermore, make sure that they stamped the right date on entry and exit. Fines are normally around US$500. Another problem you may find is that officials do not always give you the full 30 days on a visa. I have often found they count only 28 days from the date I entered, and give that as the expiry date of the visa. Talking to other backpackers, this seems to occur a lot. If you do not check, you may get to the border or airport and be fined for overstaying, while actually being in the 30-day period. They assume it is your responsibility to check that the official did not make a mistake with the date when you entered.

Fake Monks

Fake monks are a common sight in Cambodia. These will be locals, and sometimes, foreign backpackers, that dress like monks and ask for money. They will, at times, give you a fake blessing and maybe an armband. It is sometimes hard to spot a fake one from a real one. One way is to check their shoes. Monks have sandals and not closed or expensive shoes, and do not wear modern clothing such as denims under their robes. Go to a pagoda to get a real blessing from a real monk. Some of the highest monks are resident in Phnom Penh, Cambodia in Wat Ounalom.

Passport and Visa Scams

This scam can leave you in a lot of trouble. A stolen passport, and even selling your passport, is a big underground industry in SE Asia, especially in Thailand. Although many travel agencies and hostels can get visas for you, only trust large and official travel agencies. Never trust the new friend you made that claims he/she works at the embassy or has a friend there and can help you out. You may find yourself without a passport, with no way of tracking the person down. Scams also include informing you that they can get you a new passport (if yours is close to expiring), within a very short time, and then run off with your cash and old passport.

Baby For Hire

This scam is sad. Mothers rent their babies out to a con artist. They may masquerade the baby as disabled, lying in the sun at a temple, or pretend to be the mother, walking the streets asking for money to support her baby. A popular scam is called 'the milk powder scam'. The woman will not ask for money, but a tin of milk powder for her baby. You then purchase a tin from a local store thinking you are doing good, just for the women to go back to the store and exchanging the tin for a portion of the purchase price. As mentioned under volunteering, many orphanages buy or rent babies. Do not take trips to so-called orphanages, as you are just keeping this sad industry in motion.

Incense Burning in The Temples

At almost all temples, people will often have a prayer place, where monks or an old woman burn incenses. They will offer you an incense stick when you approach. When you take it, they may give you a blessing, and then expect a donation afterwards. Politely refuse the incense stick or any offer of blessing if you are not going to make a donation. It is widely accepted that if you take the incense, you are obliged to give a donation, even if they give no blessing. Moreover, not to give a donation is very rude and may result in an argument.

If you take the incense or a blessing, you have to pay. Sometimes they may offer to put a small woven armband on your wrist. It is not free, do not take it if you do not want to pay.

Can I take Your Picture?

This one is not often used, and mostly done at night to drunkards. A street kid will come up to you and offer to take your picture with your camera or cellphone. The moment you hand it over, they run like hell. Good luck in catching them. Often they will jump on a motorcycle and speed away.

Another way is for them to zoom past on a motorcycle and take your camera, while you're taking a photo, walking, or sitting in a tuk tuk. They grab cameras, cellphones, and backpacks out of your reach and speed off. Women have even been pulled off the back of a motorcycle, and dragged over the tar, when they try to rip her handbag from her. Always put your smaller bags by your feet, with one strap around your leg, and handbags between you and the driver, rather than over your shoulder or on your back. Cities to be very careful include Phnom Penh and Sihanoukville in Cambodia. If you rent a bicycle with a basket in front, put the straps of backpacks or shopping bags over the handlebars when placing the item in the basket. This will stop thieves from easily snatching the bag out of the basket.

Scam Tuk Tuks in Bangkok

From all the cities and countries I have been, it was only Bangkok that I ran into this problem. Almost every tuk tuk and motorcycle taxi tried to take me to a shop, he or a cousin owned, where they tried to get me to buy overprices stuff. Alternatively, they tell you the price to a point is X amount, and then when they drop you off say it is actually XX. Asking the local hostels owners, I was told that the best option is to take a metered cab in Bangkok instead of a tuk tuk. I found the local minibuses and the train a far better option. The standard price for a real tuk tuk is around 200 Baht an hour. Those offering 20 or 40 Baht an hour are almost 99% sure to be fake.

I Will Draw Money For You

Backpackers who like to sponge off other backpackers often employ this scam. They befriend you, telling you wonderful stories of where they have been and things they have done. They may even go on a few tours with you while serving as a guide, and offer to pay for drinks and food. At some point, they may say that they are going to draw money, normally at an ATM that does not charge a withdrawal fee, and offer to draw money for you as well. That will be the last time you see them…and your bankcard. They will draw your money as fast as they can, until you stop the card. Some are even worse. They may draw the $100 you asked, but draw an addition sum for themselves without telling you. Others do return with an ATM receipt, having drawn the right amount. Then, night after night, they slip out with your card, and empty your account. You will not even know it is them, and the moment your bank account is near empty, they just move on, with you none the wiser. Always hide your bankcard, especially when you are sleeping, and if possible put an e-mail alert on your card for whenever you draw money or use it at a pay point.

The Sponger

This friendly and social new friend will often dazzle you with wild stories, and join you for drinks and a meal. They often have expensive taste and quickly rack up a large bill. If you are lucky, they will offer to split the bill between the number of people at the table, meaning they pay far less than their share.

If you are unlucky, they will have forgotten their wallet in their room or just disappear while going to the toilet. Insist that everyone has a separate bill, or pay for your drinks and food as you go. Be wary when they disappear to the toilet close to leaving time.

Lending Money

Backpackers who sponge off other backpackers, as mentioned above, mostly employ this scam. However, here the person may tell you a sob story of how they fell victim and were robbed or lost their wallet. They will often beg you to lend them some money until they can get a new bankcard or a relative can send money via Moneygram or something similar. Although things happen to people, more often, you are going to keep paying for their bills, until you push them to pay you back, and then they just disappear. If you do want to help out, make sure the story is real, and be prepared not to get your money back.

Can I Use Your Computer?

Computer knowledgeable backpackers that sponge off others often use this one. They will borrow your laptop to just quickly check their email. Often, you will give your password to them, if you even have one on your laptop. If they can, later they will secretly take your computer and check for any websites that the passwords are saved for and log in automatically – email accounts and online banking is what they are looking for.

Actually, if they hack into your email account they can often change your online banking login. If your email program automatically downloads your email, they do not even need your email account password to change your banking login.

They then transfer all your money out, and hit the road. As the transfer was done from your computer with a valid login, there is not much you can do as the onus rests on your to keep your details safe, and not on the bank. If you do want to lend out your laptop, make sure they do not snoop around, and either give the laptop unlocked to them or change the password afterwards. Personally, I just say no.

Fake – Fake

I saw a joke saying, "You are so fake even China does not want to copy you." Realize that most things sold in SE Asia that are imported, are often fake, especially cheap items in local markets. In Thailand and Vietnam, things are normally a bit better in upmarket shops, but not always the case. Spotting a fake from the real deal is not always easy. If you are thinking of buying an expensive item, especially electronic goods, you should consider buying it back home. Even if it is not fake, you may end up with no warranty, should the item break, as few manufactures give international guarantees. Alternatively, you may be required to ship the item back to where you bought it; costing you more than the money you saved buying it in Asia.

Stolen Goods

You will notice shops selling cellphones everywhere, especially in Cambodia. Some are new, and mostly knockoffs that look like the real deal, but without the warranty. The secondhand ones are normally phones lifted from other backpackers and tourists. I heard from a few people how their brand-new iPhone and iPad, which were sold with a box, locked itself the moment they went online. It turns out they were stolen items.

Inside Tip

Not all, but some nightclubs do employ young good-looking backpackers. Their job is to lure other backpackers to their bar or nightclub. This works great because who are you going to believe, the tuk tuk driver or the fellow backpacker when they say go to a nightclub? Realize that their only job is to get you there, and get you drinking and spending money. It may not be a bad thing; it is just business, but know you will be coerced into drinking more than what is good for you or your pocket. Part of the experience of backpacking is making friends, so this is a bit of a tongue in the cheek thing, just be careful.

Double Trouble

Scams exist for both taxis, and hotels upon completion of service, they may demand that the price quoted was not per room or per ride, but per person. Always make double sure up front and get a written quotation if possible. If it sounds too good to be true, it normally is. If you are unsure of a hotel, pay up front for the room if you are happy with it, and make sure you get a slip saying you paid, stating the correct number of people. For a taxi, it may help if you record the conversation, although it does not always fly when the police arrive. Walking away without concluding the deal may result in you being arrested – better to pay up. A taxi may also demand a tip. You do not need to give any. Keep your bags with you on the seat, as scam drivers will keep the trunk locked until you pay their new price.

Is it The Right Hotel?

Make sure you are taken to the right hotel. Hotels sometimes have similar or identical names, with one being a scam. You may have booked at the expensive hotel and given your credit card details as security, only to be taken to the scam hotel by the taxi. There you will be asked to pay in cash up front, and find an inferior room as what you booked. You will be denied a refund and have a crap stay. On return to your country, you will find your credit card charged in full from the genuine hotel for a no-show booking. It is then that you will realize you were taken to a scam hotel. Get the number for the hotel you are actually booking for online, and call them when being dropped off. Also, save the pictures of the front and lobby of the hotel from the online booking to your phone, and make sure the hotel and reception are the same when dropped off by the taxi. Another way is to arrange with the hotel to pick you up at the airport or bus station, or to send a taxi if possible.

You Break it You Pay For it

Hotels sometimes run a scam where you are placed in a room with broken items (TV, air conditioner, nightstand, etch). When you check out, they may charge you for the damages. Always check the room first before agreeing to take it and do report any damages immediately to reception. If they offer you a lower rate for staying in the room, have them write down that they agree that the item was broken before you rented the room.

Chapter 22: Volunteering

Many backpackers come to SE Asia thinking they are going to do volunteer work or possibly teach English.

Here is the reality of the situation for both volunteering and teaching English for a few days or weeks.

Due to so many volunteers showing up, it has become a full-fledged industry. In addition, due to most people wanting to work with local children, a whole orphanages industry has sprung up, especially in Cambodia. These orphanages exist only to cater to foreign tourists.

Sadly, most children who are placed in orphanages in Cambodia are not orphans and have at least one living parent. Children are often bought from families to fill orphanages. So, most of the kids you see in orphanages are there because people will donate money, and not due to a real need. Furthermore, many children that pose for pictures and lay around for you to feel sorry for are kept out of school and sometimes taken to town or temples to dance and move around to impress you to donate money.

Even if you do want to teach English, ask yourself how qualified are you really? Just because you can speak English and did a month-long course in teaching, does not mean you can really teach. Also ask yourself, how are children to learn when they get a new teacher every few days, even if it is an assistant?

In truth, there are actually very few jobs in SE Asia that Asians cannot do, and if you volunteer you take away a job opportunity from a local. Also, think about it, you need to learn the ropes, so how effective can you be if you are not at least three months or longer at the job? Actually, most legit organizations will not accept volunteers who cannot stay for at least three months or more. For more information, see When Children Become Tourist Attractions site. *http://www.thinkchildsafe.org/thinkbeforevisiting/*

If you still want to volunteer, and can do it long term, check out the following organizations.

Peace Corps: *www.peacecorps.gov*
AYAD program: *www.ayad.com.au*
AusAid's VIDA program: *www.volunteering.austraining.com.au*
VSO program: *www.vso.org.uk*
PEPY Tours: *www.pepytours.com*

Chapter 23: Safety

How safe is backpacking SE Asia...really? Two questions I am often asked: are there still landmines and are there still booby traps, as seen in Vietnam war movies. Yes, there are still landmines all over SE Asia. However, tourist places have been cleared. The problem lies with remote villages and sites. As for booby traps, I think the only problem is the unexploded bombs that still lie in wait for a victim.

In general, SE Asia is safer to travel than many developed countries. You are far more likely to be robbed and shot in many cities when walking alone at night or taking a train home, than in a rural village in SE Asia. Yes, there is crime, yes tourists do get robbed and sometimes killed, but it is rare compared to the amount of tourists visiting SE Asia, and for the most part they did stupid things.

Many tips have been given in earlier chapters to help you stay save, here are a few extra ones.

Money

Do not have large amounts of money in your main wallet (anything over $100) or flash around large amounts of cash, nor brag about how much you have with you or in your bank account. In addition, if you have a number of small bills in local money, use them. You do not want a bulging wallet that gives the wrong impression. Remember, many rural villages are so poor that the people live on around $1 a day, and in the city, many workers get $60 to $150 a month. Paying and opening a wallet that bursts with money, is asking to be robbed. Have a separate wallet where you keep your passport, and put the excess money in that wallet and store it safely away.

Do not rub your wealth in other backpacker's faces. And be very careful with dorms – things do disappear if not locked up. Get a good computer lock for your laptop and lock it when you leave it alone or go to sleep. Lock your backpack in a secure place if provided, or lock the zippers and then secure the backpack to your bed by a steel cable. A bicycle seat, lock cable will do. Else go to a fishing shop and buy a steel trace and sleeves. Make loops at the ends and crimp the sleeves down to lock the loops in place.

Personally in dorms, I put my passport, wallet, bankcards, iPad and laptop, in a small day backpack, and then sleep with it by my head. The backpack's zippers are locked and the backpack itself is locked to my wrist by a steel cable.

Trains and Buses

Always put your passport, wallet, laptop, and so on in a small day bag and keep it with you. Never put it in your main backpack or in the cargo hold of a bus. When you go to the toilet, take the bag with you. On the train from Hanoi to Saigon in Vietnam (42 hours), we stopped at around 2am at a station. There was a nice Vietnamese man and his young son with me in the carriage (sleeps 4). I went to the toilet and left my backpack under my pillow, thinking they are there and asleep, and it will be okay. When I returned, the guy and his son were gone, and a lady was going through the carriage looking under the blankets of the father and son's beds. When I asked her what she was doing, she tried to sell me stale bread rolls and then quickly left the train. A minute more and she would have found my backpack. I later found the father and son outside, getting fresh air. On overnight trains, staff often crawls into the cargo hold and help themselves to items from your luggage. Never put valuables in the bags in the cargo hold.

Passports

Sometimes people pick up passports that do not belong to them by mistake. This can happen at security screening on airports, and at land border crossings (normally on buses where the conductor takes all the passports for the entire bus to the customs to be stamped). Place your passport in a passport wallet so that it stands out at airports and always make sure you have your own passport with you when you clear a security screening. As mentioned before, passport theft is a problem, so hide it when you go to bed at night or leave the room in the day.

Hotels, Apartments and Hostels

Most hotel rooms, and even backpacker places have bars in front of the windows, and secure locks on the door. This may keep someone out of your room, but not from them taking a broom or bamboo stick, with a hooked piece of wire attached, for dragging your laptop and other stuff close enough to pull it through an open window.

When you leave your room, close and lock all windows. Furthermore, draw the curtains closed if you have any to prevent people from seeing what is inside your room. Hide things so that they cannot be dragged closer if someone breaks the window. Do not leave wallets, cellphones, cameras, and laptops lying around in a room when you leave. It does happen that hotel staff become culprits and enters your hotel when you go out.

Check that one cannot open the door by sliding a window open and sticking an arm through. If the room cannot be secured, consider taking your valuables such as passport and laptop with you on day outings.

Remember, SE Asia, especially Cambodia, is one of the cheapest places to live, and one of the easiest for which to obtain a visa, or just to disappear into a small village if you want. This, coupled with the ease of getting drugs, does seem to attract some interesting characters.

Remember that being on higher floors does not protect you. Thieves can and do climb stairs and drain pipes.

On the Road

Do not place small bags and items, such as a camera, loosely down on a tuk tuk. People ride by and snatch them. Try to avoid carrying a handbag, and put your backpack on your chest when riding pillion (passenger) on a motorcycle or when standing in lines. It is easy to cut a backpack with a razorblade and empty the contents without you knowing it.

When the bus or taxi stops at roadside restaurants for a break, take your day bag, with laptop, wallet, and so on with you. Leaving it on a bus is asking for something to go missing. A minivan taxi may be more secure, but better not to take the chance, especially on night buses.

Do wear a helmet when riding on a scooter. Ask the scooter taxi for one. If you are staying for a few months and will be using motorcycle taxis a lot, then consider buying your own. They go for around $15 to $30 for a reasonable scooter helmet.

After Dark

Never walk home alone, especially women or when you are drunk. Get a tuk tuk or go as a group. Furthermore, be careful on beaches after dark when there are less than four of you, especially in Sihanoukville, Cambodia. People have been stabbed and hit over the head to be robbed of a few dollars. Also be careful of stray dogs when walking at night.

Renting a Motorcycle

Always lock the motorcycle up, and make sure it is in a secure place at night. A disc lock is not good enough at night, and perhaps not a chain lock either. You can ask the hotel or hostel if you can bring the motorcycle inside, especially if they do not have a safe place with guards. You will be liable for a new motorcycle if it gets stolen. This is a big problem in the cities of Sihanoukville and Phnom Penh.

Intoxicated

Most backpackers fall victim to crime when they are intoxicated and passed out. Unfortunately, many backpackers succumb each year to over-intoxication. Bangkok is a bit better, but in most of SE Asia, when a backpacker passed out, other backpackers and locals leave them be. At times, this has resulted in the death of the person, as they over indulged, and at times, use drugs in excess with alcohol. Please be aware, if you over indulge or overdose in most of SE Asia, there is not much they can do for you, as they lack the proper medical facilities. For your own good – avoids excessive drinking and do not experiment with drugs.

Thank you for taking the time to read **Backpacking SouthEast Asia**.

If you enjoyed this book or found it useful, I would be very grateful if you would please post a short review because your support really does make a difference. Alternatively, consider telling your friends about this book because word of mouth is an author's best friend and much appreciated.

Anton Swanepoel

If you want to contact me personally, send me an email @ *info@antonswanepoelbooks.com*

Follow this link if you want updates on new book releases by me, as well as travel tips from my blog posts.
http://antonswanepoelbooks.com/subscribe.php

About the Author

Anton Swanepoel @ Pol Pot's house on the mountains in Thailand, and on his way to Preah Vihear Temple.

For seven years, I worked as a technical diving instructor in the Cayman Islands. I am a Tri-Mix instructor in multiple agencies, and dove to over 400ft on open circuit. While on Grand Cayman, I started a passion I've always had…writing. For a number of years I saved what I could, and in Jan 2014 I moved to Siem Reap, Cambodia, to travel and focus full-time on my writing. If you want to follow my adventures, see my blog *www.antonswanepoelbooks.com/blog*.

More Books by Anton

www.antonswanepoelbooks.com

Novels
> *Laura and The Jaguar Prophecy (Book 1)*
> *Laura and The God Code (Book 2)*

Travel Diary
> *Almost Somewhere*

Peru Travel
> *Machu Picchu: The Ultimate Guide to Machu Picchu*

Travel Tips
> *Angkor Wat & Cambodia*
> *100 International Travel Tips*
> *Backpacking SouthEast Asia*

Motorbike Travel
> *Motorcycle: A Guide Book To Long Distance And Adventure Riding*
> *Motorbiking Cambodia & Vietnam*

Cambodia Travel
> *Cambodia: 50 Facts You Should Know When Visiting Cambodia*
> *Angkor Wat: 20 Must See Temples*
> *Angkor Wat Temples*
> *Angkor Wat Archaeological Park*
> *Kampot, Kep and Sihanoukville*
> *Kampot: 20 Must See Attractions*
> *Kep: 10 Must See Attractions*
> *Sihanoukville: 20 Must See Attractions*
> *Battambang: 20 Must See Attractions*
> *Phnom Penh: 20 Must See Attractions*
> *Siem Reap: 20 Must See Attractions*
> *Dangerous Loads*

Anton Swanepoel

Vietnam Travel
Vietnam: 50 Facts You Should Know When Visiting Vietnam
Vietnam Caves
Ha Long Bay
The Perfumed Pagoda
Phong Nha Caves

Thailand
Thailand: 50 Facts You Should Know When Visiting Thailand
Bangkok: 20 Must See Attractions
Ayutthaya: 20 Must See Attractions
The Great Buddha

Laos
Vientiane: 20 Must See Attractions

South Africa
South Africa: 50 Facts You Should Know When Visiting South Africa
Pretoria: 20 Must See Attractions
Freedom Park
Union Buildings
The Voortekker Monument Heritage Site
The Cradle of Humankind Heritage Site

Diving Books
The Art of Gas Blending
Dive Computers
Gas Blender Program
Deep and Safety Stops, and Gradient Factors
Diving Below 130 Feet

Writing Books
Supercharge Your Book Description

Self Help Books
Ear Pain
Sea and Motion Sickness

Made in the USA
Lexington, KY
27 April 2017